PAUL FRE

D0453980

How to Develop
a Tithing Church

How to Develop a Tithing Church

CHARLIE W. SHEDD

Abingdon Press

NASHVILLE

HOW TO DEVELOP A TITHING CHURCH

Copyright © 1961 by Abingdon Press

13th Printing 1985

All rights in this book are reserved.
No part of the book may be reproduced in any
manner whatsoever without written permission of
the publisher except brief quotations embodied in
critical articles or reviews. For information address
Abingdon Press, Nashville, Tennessee.

ISBN 0-687-17798-7

MANUFACTURED BY THE PARTHENON PRESS AT
NASHVILLE, TENNESSEE, UNITED STATES OF AMERICA

To

Leo Frohlich

devoted layman, peerless planner, and friend extraordinary
with whom it was the author's privilege
to share the earliest developments
of this program

Contents

I

History and Results

TEN YEARS AGO I SAT IN THE STUDY OF A FINE CHURCH. IT WAS "Loyalty Week" and our men were out in the parish knocking on doors. Pledge Sunday was over and they were "cleaning up." This was a necessary conclusion to raising a budget.

Ours was a "great" church by many standards. It boasted an active program which required big money to staff and operate its good works. We had laid a careful foundation for this drive and the concerted push now moved toward a healthy oversubscription.

But there were some strange goings on in the mind of this pastor. From out of the inmost chambers where voices are silenced in life's busy rushing, there came now some telling questions. They began with a phrase extracted from one of the Budget letters: "If only everyone in this church would give fifty cents more per week, we could make it without too much hardship on anyone."

A check of the pledges revealed that there were many to whom this had been a successful appeal. But the voices asked, "What do you mean, you could make 'it'? You've made your budget, but is this *your 'it'* or *the Lord's 'it'* for the lives of these people? And how does your 'without too much hardship on anyone' appear against the background of Christ on his cross?"

I interrupted the inner needling and argued: "But look how much better we are doing than they did in the last pastorate. And our average is several dollars above that denomination across the street. Aren't the officers pleased, and didn't we have chairs in the aisles last Sunday?"

At this point my Holy Visitor began hurling scripture straight into my argument:

"Be not conformed to this world." "Set your affections on things above, not on things on the earth." "Whosoever will come after me, let him deny himself, and take up his cross, and follow me." "To what purpose is the multitude of your sacrifices unto me?" "Christ gave himself for us, that he might redeem us from all iniquity, and purify unto himself a peculiar people, zealous of good works."

Sometimes a man knows when he's beaten, so I closed the door to my study and went home to my wonderful wife, who knows when to soothe her man with loving care, well-worded praise, and a warm meal. The evening with my laughing family was "balm in Gilead."

But the next morning *he* was there again; and when I told him he had won that round, he gave me specific directions for my next move. He guided me to the store of a successful young merchant who, much to my surprise, had been visited with similar insights.

Leo was chairman of the "big gifts" section of the campaign, and it was to his superb work that we owed much of our success. Through his efforts some of our major contributors had doubled their pledges, and others had been persuaded to "up" their annual amount to "take up the slack of those who might not subscribe fifty cents more per week."

He handed me a letter as we sat in the little room at the back of his store. I sensed that he was a bit uncomfortable. It was only a brief note from the chairman of our local board, who, himself, was one of the most prosperous gentlemen in our commonwealth. The letter read:

> Dear Leo:
>
> I want you to know that I think your handling of our "big gifts" campaign in the church this year was one of the smoothest operations I have ever seen. This should do much to continue our reputation as a real "go-getter" in our denomination. Congratulations.
>
> X
> _____
> CHAIRMAN OF THE BOARD

I looked at Leo. He looked at me. We looked to the Lord together, and out of that experience there was born the "Program Toward a Tithing Church."

It wasn't easy. When you appear before the joint boards of a church which has just completed its most successful canvass ever; when you present the idea that something may yet be wrong, they are apt to give you the "Look at the man with two heads!" treatment.

We outlined what we called a "Twenty-Year Program of Stewardship Training," and asked for a committee to study the

11

possibilities. This group would make recommendations back to the officers, so they would be perfectly safe in such an appointment.

I will never forget that meeting. It was held in the sanctuary with some ninety men present. They had come together to hear the final report of the budget drive, and this was a time for loud hand clapping, nodding the head, and wide smiles of satisfaction.

But there was something else! We have a Labrador retriever at our house. Deacon is a beautiful yellow dog, and when he senses danger out there in the dark, the golden hairs go straight up all the way down his back. I am told that he does this by instinct, and that it is a natural reaction to fear in this particular breed.

There were at this meeting some very fine officers who, when they sensed the full impact of what was to come, reacted by instinct in true Deacon fashion. These were wise men; some of them were among the best financiers I have known. Wherever their dollars were involved they had a natural sense by which they could look into the future and foretell things to come. With each mention of the words "percentage giving," "tithing," and "New Testament stewardship" their opposition mounted, and the entire project was nearly destroyed before it began.

But there were others who had been visited by the same Holy Caller who had talked to the two of us in his unique way. We were not alone in our dissatisfaction with the "super" job which we had accomplished. Others also had sensed for some time that there must be something better than the one big push each year. There just might be a program superior to the annual high-powered budget drive.

The committee was appointed by a majority vote. It gave itself to thoughtful study and careful preparation. After numerous meetings and serious prayer it reported back to the joint boards which had launched it on a choppy sea. (Each denomination has its own legal procedure for such appointment. Some of the details of approach are not set forth extensively here due to denominational variances. Suffice it to say that each local church does well to follow carefully its proper steps. It also proves wise to specify the committee's responsibilities and indicate to whom they should report as their work proceeds.)

For a time it appeared that the little boat would never make it home. The opposition had also been meeting over morning coffee and their spokesman made a convincing appeal to let well-enough alone. He began with, "Once there was a goose which laid some golden eggs," and described the foolish farmer who slew the bird to discover its magic. He pictured a now "full house" at Sabbath worship diminished to empty pews by excessive emphasis on an embarrassing subject. This was a good man speaking. He was a pillar. He was incisive. He was sincere. But he was outvoted.

So the Program Toward a Tithing Church became a reality when a wise and gentle member moved to give it a twelve-month try.

At the end of one year it became a permanent fixture, and for nearly nine years it was my privilege to study its leavening influence on an important congregation.

The Results

It is quite impossible to measure spiritual intangibles by statistics. The writer has seen amazing results, not only in the personal spiritual development of individuals, but in new in-

terest in the church's entire effort. The words of Jesus, "where
your treasure is there will your heart be also," have become living
reality in the cases of many whose realignment of financial stewardship has led to dedication of time and talents as well. Growth
in grace can never be defined in the limited media of words.
Pastoral ethics would forbid the revelation of some soul-
accountings which resulted as the years went by. Perhaps the
reader will accept this letter as evidence that good things happened in human hearts through this development. I quote from
a man who sat as a young officer that night when the Program
Toward a Tithing Church was born.

I went home bothered. M_____ and I had been dollar-a-week
givers through all our marriage and this was the first time we had
been forced to rethink our giving habits. Over our coffee we got
out our budget, our check stubs, and our feeble bank account. We
put down on paper what tithing would do to us and to say that we
were "all shook up" is putting it mildly. We couldn't do anything
that crazy and we dismissed it with a big fat "No." But every Sunday there was that notice in the bulletin, and once I was even asked to
give a talk about "percentage giving" at our church-school class.
You can imagine how I felt about that. What I said was that the
Bible says it is a good thing if you can do it. I was glad there was
no time for questions and answers.

Well, to make a long story short, it finally got to us. We decided
to start out with 4 per cent and see where that would take us. I
guess we picked four just because we had four children. So we
started and you know what happened. Each year when budget time
came round we upped our percentage until you know the rest. No,
we didn't make a million, but we have done all right, and we
wouldn't go back to haphazard giving for anything in the world. It

isn't what happened to us financially when we decided to enter this partnership with God. Instead, it seems like this was the beginning of relating all our lives to him in a specific way. The things which have happened in our hearts since that day are much more important than what happened in our pocketbooks. There have been some tough times, some ups and downs, but we both feel that the Lord has blessed us in a way which would never have been possible without *someone* or *something* forcing us to get right with him *somewhere*. We are deeply grateful to our church for this teaching.

Financial results are easier to measure. During nine years of the Program Toward a Tithing Church in that congregation we saw the operating budget move from $19,000 annually to $90,000. This is an increase of more than 400 per cent. During this same period, due to removals in a major industry, the growth in membership was only 26 per cent. In this same nine-year period the church built a $650,000 building and paid $400,000 in cash on that project.

Even more significant is the record in benevolence giving which took place during the period described. In nine years the benevolence contributions of that church rose from 13 per cent of the budget to 50 per cent. (It is the studied opinion of those who had experience with the program that increased giving to others must be an integral part of the movement. People who raise their percentages are due an accounting of their money's use, and they will respond with a growing zest when they know that they are hereby winning the world for Christ.)

From this church I was called to a different pastorate. This is one of the hundreds of new congregations dotting the landscape in the suburbs of America's large urban centers.

Obviously, one of the first programs presented to the boards of the church for their consideration was a replica of that Program Toward a Tithing Church which I had seen do great things for an historically established people.

Records here are inconclusive because of the limited time involved. Spiritually speaking, the same thing holds. Lives are changed and hearts opened to a new sense of Christian responsibility as new members come under the influence of the Program Toward a Tithing Church which we have adapted to our needs.

Twelve months after the program was launched here we had a building fund and operating expense canvass which resulted in the following interesting data: 193 pledging families subscribed $200,000 toward the first unit of a new building (36 month pledges). In addition, these same givers undertook an $80,000 annual budget.

In the fourth year of the program with a membership now grown to 1,000, our year's budget totaled $170,000. Of this, $50,000 was for debt retirement and building costs, with the remainder divided $60,000 to operating and $60,000 to benevolences.

This church has no known millionaires. It has many young, salaried families who are buying their homes, plus a sizable number of rising young executives with excellent income. It has some retired couples, and many people coming into its membership whose stewardship habits in their former churches are poor enough to make our officers shudder when they consider the future obligations of our work.

It is precisely at this point that temptation comes to those directing the program. Panic seizes all of us at times and especially when our faith wanes. No program is good enough to elicit the solid support of everyone. Some will point to figures and cry

16

out that we are bound for catastrophe. At such times there will be others of long vision and deep confidence who will "breathe through the heats" their own ability to wait on the Lord. Officers who have had experience in crash tactics elsewhere will insist that the old way is best. It takes depth of foundation to build high buildings, and the stewardship planners of a local church do well to promote an accompanying program in spiritual development to match their new concepts of church finance.

In addition to the serious commitments which go with a large building project, this church has a dollar-for-dollar benevolence program. (In our denomination a church is considered a dollar-for-dollar work when for every dollar spent in the local operating budget it sends a matching dollar for work outside the local parish.) This necessitates an unusually heavy load during the first few years when the church is developing a staff and a budget to handle a fast-growing membership.

It should be noted, however, that although such a benevolence development is very expensive in outgo, it is also a mighty source of intake. God has a way of filling those places which are emptied for his occupancy. We find that certain people shy away from a congregation with such a stewardship commitment. But it is also our experience that for each of these there are several others who affiliate here because of this program. Some of our members drive a considerable distance in order to have a part in this movement. It is a continual challenge to put down pride in a dollar-for-dollar undertaking and replace this with humble gratitude for God's goodness and our responsibility to the Kingdom. But it would be the author's judgment that the quiet feeling of doing what ought to be done is a major factor in evange

17

lism with us. In other words, it not only costs, it also pays. Such a program serves as a filter at the entrance, but it also acts as a funnel by which God is poured out to the world, and room is made for more of his presence in the soul of the church. It is spiritually true that the best way to be filled with God's presence is to be emptied of self.

As previously stated, we do not have enough time behind us to present figures which could be documented with time. To date it looks as if the benevolence commitment and stewardship program are part of a whole. But it suffices to say that most of the officers are wholeheartedly for both the benevolence approach and the long-range financial stewardship training. It is evident that many of us are being searched and challenged to spiritually test our giving, both as a church and as individuals.

II

Theology for Christian Stewardship

"WE ARE NOT CONCERNED WITH YOUR SHARE OF OUR BUDGET! What matters is God's share of your income."

This is an official statement of our Program Toward a Tithing Church. Our people see it often in their Sunday bulletins and in congregational correspondence. It is given from pulpit and classroom. It is carried in our local church paper. It is told to prospects and explained to members. It is frequently introduced into private conversation when the life of the church is discussed. It is used often by our officers who have committed themselves to consider it seriously on a personal basis and to use it at opportune times in their leadership.

Yet this is only the beginning. This pivotal phrasing of our stewardship program is designed to seize the attention of the church member's soul. It seeks to force him to ask, "What part of my income belongs to the Lord?"

Behind this question lies a deep study of the Word of God in both Old and New Testaments. Every serious steward will be vitally interested in the query, "What does the Bible say about my stewardship?" As he seeks for an answer to this question, the Christian naturally will concern himself with Christ as the Living Word to the individual disciple. He will seek honest answers to such matters as, "Did Jesus believe in the tithe?" He will also come on the New Testament conviction that Christ is for all the world.

It is from such a study as this that we have developed our Program Toward a Tithing Church. The terms "proportionate giving" and "percentage giving" used so frequently in our approach are not mere catch phrases for promotional purposes. They are for us the logical outcome of what we believe the Bible says to us concerning modern-day giving.

We present here the results of this study under the following outline:

1. The Biblical Foundation of Christian Stewardship
     Christ as the personal word of God
     Christ and the question of tithing
     Christ for all the world
2. The Local Church Applies These Teachings
     Proportionate giving
     Why the term "percentage"?

At the conclusion of this chapter we list reasons why we believe specific directions are imperative. Following this, we have enumerated certain dangers which we have found in our own thinking and in the popular presentations of our day.

THE BIBLICAL FOUNDATION OF CHRISTIAN STEWARDSHIP

T. A. Kantonen in his *Theology for Christian Stewardship* drives a long nail in the coffin of man-made plans:

It makes a vast difference in the nature of the stewardship appeal whether it is one man drawing upon his ingenuity and resourcefulness to interest another man in a good cause, or whether it is God himself who lays claim to a man's whole life, saying, "I am the Lord thy God; thou shalt have no other Gods . . . before me."

Any honest church will present only those claims which it believes to be God speaking out of his Word. This will require diligent Bible study by the pastor and leaders. In the case of those churches with official connections at points outside the local church, it will demand careful perusal of denominational declarations and historical standards.

But even these things are only fully understood in the light of the Living Word.

Christ as the personal Word of God

The gospel affirms of Jesus that "the Word became flesh and dwelt among us" (John 1:14). The Christian Church must not only see itself as steward of a Book; it must also recognize that it is to be the reflection of a living Lord who speaks through it and builds his Kingdom by its work.

This is why any program of good stewardship training must start with the concept of "allness." Jesus taught that nothing but a wholehearted response to God would do. "Thou shalt love the Lord thy God with all thy heart, and with all thy soul, and with all thy strength, and with all thy mind; and thy neighbor as thyself" (Luke 10:27) is the Master's own summary of the extent of man's obligation to his Maker.

The Living Word thus draws his circle about our total life and claims our full existence as his own.

Stewardship planning within the Christian Church, having

21

set itself squarely on such a base, will proceed to concern itself seriously with what is most acceptable to Christ. Paul said, "We make it our aim to please him" (II Cor. 5:9).

Here we have the basic reason for all Christian stewardship. In Old Testament times men sought to satisfy God largely because they were afraid. In the New Testament mind the passionate desire to please him is a response to love. "God hath not given us the spirit of fear; but of power and of love" (II Tim. 1:7). This is a glorious truth for which the Christian Church may sing in constant gratitude.

When it dawns on the individual that God loves him and sent his Son to draw this disciple to life eternal with him, there will be an inevitable facing up to personal responsibilities. As he moves into a full awareness of what Christ has done for him, he will be overcome with the awesome truth that all he is, plus all he has, is none too much for such a Lord. He will want to yield his all, he will continually consider how he can yield even more, and he will listen to the voice of God within his heart directing his fuller surrender.

Christ and the question of tithing

Jesus mentioned the tithe only twice. In the parable of the Pharisee and the publican our Lord quoted the pious one with these words, "I give tithes of all that I possess" (Luke 18:12). In his woes to the pompous, Jesus warned, "Woe to you, scribes and Pharisees, hypocrites! for ye pay tithe of mint and anise and cummin, and have omitted the weightier matters of the law, judgment, mercy, and faith: these ought ye to have done, and not to leave the other undone" (Matt. 23:23).

There is considerable variance among the scholars as to Jesus' full intent at the point of tithing. Some argue that his denunciation of the Pharisees is tantamount to a negative attitude toward tithing. Certain interpreters hold that the word "ought" refers only to "judgment, mercy and faith" and not to the tithe. The fact is that the Greek interpretation of the verse leaves much question for one who wants unquestionable proof in either direction.

A popular rendition of these verses is presented by Holmes Rolston in his book *Stewardship in the New Testament Church.* Dr. Rolston holds:

When we view this casual reference to the tithe by Jesus in the midst of a passage which centers in His stern denunciation of the legalism of the Pharisees, we cannot feel that this passage can be properly interpreted as expressing either the approval or the disapproval by Jesus of the tithe as a principle of Christian giving.

Dr. Rolston is a brilliant scholar whose book generally is a masterpiece in interpreting the New Testament mind. But no book contains all truth, and some of us feel that we must give more careful consideration to these words of Christ than to dismiss them as neutral ground in the mind of our Lord.

That Jesus was pointing up more important duties than the tithe is unquestionable. This does not infer, however, that he thereby was mitigating man's attention to his stewardship of small things. If proper stewardship guidance insists that Christ wants our all, this must mean things minute as well as mighty. One of the long recognized scholars of the New Testament sums up this conclusion when he says,

Their carefulness about trifles is not condemned, but sanctioned.

23

It is the neglect of essentials which is denounced as fatal. *It is not correct to say that Christ abolished the ceremonial part* of the law while retaining the moral part.[1]

The careful student discovers that the "ought to have done" statement may have been added by Matthew. This is known because certain ancient manuscripts omit it altogether. Yet this possibility does not authorize disregard of the opposite possibility that they may have been Jesus' own words, and he may have intended them for our instruction.

With so much argument among the scholars and so many questions as to positive meanings, what is a proper approach? It is our conclusion that whereas this was one of the few places where Jesus used the word "ought," we must give serious heed and ask him, as the Living Word, to reveal his desires personally to us at this point.

Christ for all the world

Another reason for serious stewardship training is that it lifts the churchman's eye above the narrow confines of local needs. It will be readily apparent to any reader of the New Testament that Jesus had big things in mind. In his earliest recorded words we find the statement, "I must be about my Father's business," and in his final instructions to the disciples he said, "Go ye into all the world."

Moving on into the sacred writings we discover that the apostle Paul was possessed with a holy passion for "the furtherance of the gospel," and church history since that day is the record of a movement for world domination by Christ.

---

[1] Alfred Plummer, *The International Critical Commentary* (New York: Charles Scribner's Sons, 1910), p. 311. Italics mine.

A study of the New Testament church offers many arguments for voluntary offerings in God's house today. The original purpose of these offerings was to relieve the saints who needed assistance and to support the work of those who carried the gospel.

The concerned Christian will sit long before such queries as these: "How shall they hear without a preacher? And how shall they preach, except they be sent?" (Rom. 10:14-15). This same follower, if he is intent on doing the will of the Lord, listens seriously when the gospel commands, "Pray ye therefore the Lord of the harvest, that he will send forth labourers into his harvest" (Matt. 9:38). He asks himself the pointed question, "Am I, by my stewardship practices, doing what Christ wants from me to win the world?"

This is another major reason for careful planning on the part of the church as it seeks to train its people in Christian giving.

The Local Church Applies These Teachings

In our congregation we use the title Program Toward a Tithing Church. As the reader will see, this is not because we hold the tithe to be the maximum end of Christian giving. In brief, we believe that the New Testament churchman will ponder the tithe in this light:

The tithe is a time-honored practice which has glorified God in the lives of many people, both Christian and unchristian. In the first biblical accounts of man's relation to God, the tithe was law. In the coming of Christ, man moved from a period of law to a period of grace. The response of the Christian soul will be one of earnest desire to yield its all to him who gave his all for us. As we consider tithing in the light of Bible history, and in the practice of many Christians today, we will discover that the tithe is not dead, nor should it be, but we must also go beyond the tithe and give careful consideration to the New Testament teaching of proportionate giving. Out of this background we believe in calling people to percentage giving, in order that they may have a specific starting point on a road which encompasses the doctrine of tithing and moves beyond it to the total surrender of all they have and all they are. As such, we are concerned with Jesus' attitude toward the tithe. Here we discover that we must let Christ, the Living Word, speak to us personally. This is the aim of all our planning.[1]

It is obvious, then, that any program which seeks to develop a tithing church must do so on larger grounds than "Ten per cent is what Christ wants." We have already said that what Christ wants is total commitment of life to him and a *full* response to divine love.

Proportionate giving

Where the Old Testament society was expected to tithe, there is conclusive evidence that the New Testament church was instructed in proportionate giving. Paul, in detailing the collection for the saints, sums up this teaching in his letter to the church at Corinth with the directive, "Upon the first day of the week let every one of you lay by him in store, as God hath prospered him" (I Cor. 16:2).

This is not the place for a lengthy treatment of New Testament stewardship teaching. It is enough to say that the best biblical scholarship and the finest writings in this field indicate sufficient New Testament grounds for the church to develop a program which emphasizes:

[1] For a concise outline which we publish for our people's direction see Appendix I.

Proportionate giving.

Regular weekly giving.

Giving the pledged amount first.

Sacrificial giving.

Cheerful giving.

Giving under a sense of obligation to care for the needs of others.

And above all, giving as a result of yielding the entire soul as a response to the love of God in Christ.

Why the term "percentage"?

In the particular program described here the words "percentage giving" are used in preference to the term "proportionate giving" because an actual check reveals that they are better understood by the modern mind. In our common vernacular of "interest," "margin of profit," "up two points," and "selling on commission," we have found that men and women of today's church are more specifically challenged when we say, "Set aside a definite percentage of your income and covenant with the Lord for that," than they are challenged when we say, "Be a proportionate giver" or "Give as God has prospered you."

Therefore the term "percentage giving" is used in preference to other wording, because it is well understood. It has the advantage of taking the hearer out of the abstract into the definite. At almost every point, we have had many questions in carrying out this program, but no one in our experience has ever asked, "What does it mean to set aside a percent of my income?" We do not attempt to prove percentage giving as a scriptural mode of stewardship. We do repeatedly say, "This is a place to begin in your response to the love of God. This is one way to be specific as you face the demands of full commitment. This dedication is a symbol that you have recognized the divine source of all your possessions. It is a banner of your partnership with God."

THE NECESSITY OF BEING SPECIFIC

It was a sharp wag who observed of the speaker, "He electrified and he edified, but he never specified."

We believe that church members must settle down at some specific points in their surrender to the Lord. We urge our people to covenant with God for a definite percentage. We believe this approach has scriptural foundations in the life of the early Church. But we also believe it is essential to Christian growth for these reasons:

1. *Christianity is based on commitment.* The over-all dedication of life to Christ must be followed by definite changes. The serious disciple will want direction. As he builds his launching base for the Christian life, he will respond to guidance when he can be made to see that it will benefit his growth in Christ.

2. Proportionate giving not only has a strong New Testament basis, but *full Christian stewardship involves a right sense of balance of all life's aspects.* It requires proper judgment. It forces careful attention to comparisons between what the Christian spends on himself and what he gives to Kingdom causes.

3. *Inadequate challenges* are one of the most serious problems of concerned churchmen. Pastors and interested laymen are aware that many joining the church have stewardship habits which can only be overcome by careful planning and constant repetition. Our evangelistic zeal for new souls in the Lord must never overlook fuller conversion of those within the fellowship. Marginal membership shows up nowhere more clearly than at the "collection" plate, and the "morning offering" is too often

28

nothing but that. If some photoscopic ray could be installed in our beautiful houses of worship, how often would it pick up such thoughts as these at moments for the offering: "I wouldn't want to live in a community without churches—I certainly expect to do my part. Sometime when I get my bills caught up I'm going to try this 'tithing business'. . . . The church is always asking for money. . . . I suppose someone has to pay the preacher. . . . I should be giving more but a man has to think of his future."

Such revelation might be startling in the average church on any given Sabbath. But it might be even more alarming at those points where the worshiper dropped his contribution into the plate with so little thought that it registered no reaction. The church which cares will face this great void with a definite plan in its hand.

4. *Church people need direction.* The pressures of modern society pose a real threat to a Christian steward. Demands from the economic realities of most church families are a constant menace to indefinite commitments. Whenever a follower of Christ is unsystematic in his giving habits, he is vulnerable to postponements and subject to ruts which continue far down the road. The church which cares for its people will plan and carry out a ministry of direction which is designed to help the members grow in the Lord.

There are those who will resent what they call "the church's intrusion on privacy," but for every one of these there will be many hearts sincerely grateful for a program which says, "Start someplace as a recognition of God's claim on all your living. Then grow as Christ calls you on."

DANGERS TO BE CONSIDERED

The church which seeks an honest approach to stewardship teaching will be alert to some flaws in modern-day considerations of tithing. There are false motives which must be repeatedly pointed out in the thoughts of others and in our own thinking as immature Christians.

One of these is the "give-to-get" theme. It is true that Jesus repeatedly taught the law of reaping what is sown. He clearly revealed that attitudes and actions have a way of returning to their original base. But Christian stewardship which is generous out of a motive of personal gain is hardly worthy of the name Christian.

Jesus taught that we are to yield our lives to him with no reservations. He also made it evident that such a life would be the epitome of blessing. But we are to give for him, not for us, and this point must be continually checked if we would be as we should.

Jesus made it clear that God's blessings are never wages for keeping God's commandments. The love of God is a continuing thing which seeks us out, and he who understands the gospel knows that Christ came to personalize God's constant search for his own. The Scriptures make it plain that the Father's love waits to bless us above all that we ask or think.

The teaching of Christian stewardship is not for the intent of showing men how to buy God's grace. It is rather to teach men how to respond to a grace which is so complete that "Eye hath not seen, nor ear heard, neither have entered into the heart of man, the things which God hath prepared for them that love him" (I Cor. 2:9). This verse is rightly associated both with life's daily blessings and with the glories of life everlasting.

Christian stewardship must ever be measured against the large background of eternity. The New Testament is replete with promises of endless joy to those who keep the faith. But the alert Christian will continually remember that he serves the Lord not that he might have the ever-present love of God forever but that the ever-present love of God might forever have him.

This is a major point of concern for church stewardship program planners. "Give in order to get" is a trap into which laymen and ministers alike may easily fall. Nothing but serious study and careful guidance can present these facts in their Christian light.

A second serious threat concerns the mistaken idea that ten per cent might relieve us of further obligation. The Christian who tithes never does so because he believes he is thereby discharging life's full expectancy. Rather, he does it because he believes Christ wants him to do this as a definite symbol of his confession that all life belongs to the Lord.

Even the legalistic Old Testament tither did not think of his tithes as freeing him from doing more. When the term "tithes and offerings" was fully understood, it required ten per cent as "belonging unto the Lord" and the offering as an over-and-above gift in addition to the tithe. It would be a mistake for any Christian to think of the tithe as a maximum. Even our principles of taxation follow the line of increasing percentages in the higher income brackets. There are Christian men and women who, in response to the guiding grace of God, have gone beyond the tithe as he has called them to ever-deepening commitment of their all to him.

Another danger of tithing training within the local congrega-

31

tion focuses on those who are honestly led not to tithe. The church which lays it on the hearts of its members to seek divine guidance in such matters, must allow room for those who are honestly not guided in this direction. It is possible that there are people whose full dedication to Christ might lead them to contributions less than ten per cent of their income. Family situations vary, and personal problems have a way of becoming extremely intricate in certain situations. It is conceivable that certain gifts could be perfect in the sight of the Lord even though they are not so in the sight of men. The fact that some church members use this thought as a door of retreat when they should not does not excuse the church from declaring this truth where and when it should.

Another allied danger to the foregoing is the idea that stewardship concerns only the giving of money. Although this book deals especially with the economic phases of Christian stewardship, those planning an over-all training program will insist on repeated emphasis at other points.

There is the stewardship of *time,* where a Christian must continually check his doings against his full response to the love of God.

There is also the important stewardship of *possessions.* The man who has given his church a generous percentage of the funds from which he purchased his automobile is not relieved of putting that car daily at the Lord's disposal. Every time he takes the wheel, with each trip to his office, anywhere he goes he must remember that what he sometimes thinks he owns is really owned by God.

Again, the stewardship of *abilities* has ample New Testament call from the Lord who said, "Every one to whom much is given, of him will much be required" (Luke 12:48). Whether he has much talent or little talent, the dedicated Christian will concern himself earnestly with the stewardship of all he has to the Lord.

Tithing as a way of Christian stewardship must be understood in the light of these facts. Tithing is an ancient practice which helps some Christians to express in a steady, defined way their full response to the love of God in Christ. It must be personally and seriously considered at all points in the still small whispers and loud sounding voices of the Living Word.

III

Four Basic Attitudes Toward
Church Finance

ONE OF OUR YOUNG CANVASSERS WAS HIMSELF SO DEDICATED TO
percentage giving that he once returned a check for five hundred dollars when it was offered to him. The man who was
turned down later became an ardent enthusiast himself. He describes the incident like this:

So I give the kid my check for five hundred and sit back waiting
for his smile. Imagine my surprise when he hands it back to me and
says, "Mr. _____, we would much rather you would promise God a certain percentage of all you receive, and keep that promise, than to accept your check for this amount."

Such action may seem drastic but it is understandable against
the background of our Program Toward a Tithing Church.
There are four basic attitudes toward church finance to which we
hold. In addition to serving as cornerstones, they offer us some
sharp check points.

1. We seek to develop a program of church finance which will be focused on the soul and not on the purse.

We strive always to center on the fact that Christian stewardship at all points is primarily a matter of aligning the heart with Christ. It is our hope to make all of our statements, all of our claims, and all of our challenges a part of the church's call to full Christian commitment.

The giving of time and service to the Lord's work is important. The use of talents and abilities is vital. The giving of money is a necessary part of life with Christ. Yet all of these must be motivated, not from a springboard of "You should be doing something," or "We need your help so badly," but from a heart which seeks to give its all to Christ who gave his all.

We attempt to keep this basic fact constantly before us in all our planning. "Out of the heart are the issues of life," and the giver of funds which come from the purse alone is only half way home to the higher alignment which redeems and saves. For this reason we seek souls which are won to Christ and not purses committed to a particular practice. This aim keeps us "centering-down" on the Lord.

2. Our second basic attitude is summed up in these words: *We seek to develop a program of church finance which will be focused on what the Lord wants and not what the church needs.*

One of the big "don'ts" of our doing is brought to light often. Our evangelism callers, church officers, those who speak for the program, and members of the church are urged to refrain from saying, "We want you to be a percentage giver so the church will prosper." We earnestly avoid such statements as, "If everyone would tithe see where the church would be!" It is true that the church would be free of financial worries if every one of its members tithed. But if each one tithed with nothing more than legal-istic obedience to a rule, the church might meet the same wrath of the Lord which rained on the Pharisees who tithed for show and looked for reward.

It is for this reason that we urge our people to study the Scriptures for light on their stewardship. We refer them often to the Bible for direction. We call them constantly to consider the Old Testament law of tithing as they ask Christ, the Living Word, what he would have them do. We keep always before our members the New Testament call to proportionate giving.

It is our continual refrain that "The wants of the Lord are more important than the needs of the church."

3. We attempt to develop a program which will be *projected over a long range and not limited to the requirements of a yearly budget.*

This is not a "drive" or a "campaign." It has none of the marks of hurry. It avoids crash tactics. Continual repetition replaces emergency appeals, and the whole movement is conceived as a continuing process. It may take twenty years to reach the goal— but since the twenty years will pass anyway, we move forward in the faith that we will reap in due season if we faint not.

We try to see our budget as an appendage and not as the body. "Try" is the proper word. It takes real effort to think in such a framework. Voices of the world and the ingenious tech-niques of the speedy modern mind are very appealing, but we believe that sometimes the most certain way home may be the long way around. One of the theories on which we work is that often the surest way to get a big job done is to do a little bit thoroughly and regularly.

4. The church member may become a follower of Christ in that

moment when he makes his first commitment, but to become a full follower may take a full lifetime. This is why *our program moves away from demands for set amounts to calls for "growth in grace."*

It is evident that no weakening of the Christian call could satisfy the Christ who said, "If any man would come after me, let him deny himself, and take up his cross, and follow me" (Matt. 16:24). The church which makes no demands cannot be true to the Lord whom it seeks to serve.

But at some points the church has sinned in its attempt to interpret the call of the Lord for all men. We believe our proper challenge is never a demand for "so much money to satisfy Jesus," but rather a call to "give your heart to Christ and let him direct your living."

This is another reason why we emphasize percentage giving. We not only believe it is true to New Testament teaching; we also hold that it is a media whereby the Christian can "grow in grace." We aim for a tithing church, but not because we believe tithing is the apex of Christian giving. We believe tithing is an ancient practice which has been a rich blessing to Christian and non-Christian alike. We believe Christ wants to speak to us personally about it. We believe no Christian can dismiss it without serious consideration and diligent study of the Scriptures.

But we also know that tithing is a frightening word to some. There are people joining our church who are not ready to tithe. Beginners in the spiritual life may need to crawl before they can walk, or to walk before they can run. Conversion is an immediate experience, but it is also a continuing development as the soul responds to new insights.

Christ comes into that heart which accepts him, but as he lives in that life he opens up new wastelands to his development. We remember always that true Christian stewardship of funds may be a process of surrender between the individual and the Lord.

ANOTHER DON'T

As stated previously, "Don't number one" for our workers is: "Don't say, 'You ought to tithe so the church will prosper.'"

Our second "Don't" is: Don't argue. Common questions associated with percentage giving and tithing talk are, "Do you mean I should figure my income before taxes or after taxes?" "Should I count what I give to Red Cross and other charities?" "Are you talking about gross or net?" The list grows large.

Our official answer is, "Your percentage giving is between you and your Lord. You decide with him what is right for your right relationship to him who gave his all for you." Many of these questions have no answer applicable to all cases. Circumstances differ in individual lives. We urge our people to be ready to testify to their own habits as they are led by divine guidance, but never to wrangle. Discussion of percentage giving and tithing is good, but argument in our experience gains nothing.

PATIENCE

As previously indicated, a prime requisite for such a program as this is the ability to "wait on the Lord." It is true that we sometimes panic as we view our mounting financial responsibilities. In our particular work, only the treasurer knows what each family gives, but as the pledges come in with the passing weeks, his monthly statements report their average to the boards. There

38

is a moment allowed for cold chills, and then we remind ourselves that these only reflect the bad stewardship habits of previous church connections or the first feeble steps of new Christians. We are *concerned* if after one year in our church, these
families give indication that our stewardship training is not getting through to them. We need to be alarmed if at the end of
two years there is still no upward trend in the case at hand.

It is true that there will be individual problems in every
gathering-together of God's children. Certain folks have circumstances which make improbable any more than token giving,
and this goes on forever in some lives. There are also people
whose mind is so thoroughly set that they may never be moved
by us. These too are sheep of the Good Shepherd and it was a
wise chairman of our board who said to his men at their first
training seminar, "I hope we will never get into habits of thinking, 'These people are *worth* a lot to us.' Everyone is worth
everything to the Lord, and that should be our attitude."

An accompanying instruction in mental elasticity is paramount
for those who guide the stewardship program of any people.
A good churchman will seek to develop the long-suffering of the
Lord "whose mercy is from everlasting to everlasting."

IV

Plan of Operation

CONSTANT REPETITION IN AN ATTRACTIVE MANNER IS THE UNDER-lying technique of our Program Toward a Tithing Church. When a swamp is to be filled with stones, many loads are required beneath the surface before the results appear on top. "By long forbearing is a prince persuaded, and a soft tongue breaketh the bone" (Prov. 25:15).

Bad habits in giving, long histories of casual stewardship, and minds already set in neglect of the Lord are broken sometimes by catastrophic events. This is good, and any time a soul is converted to Christian practices there is occasion for rejoicing.

Those church leaders who believe that tithing is a requisite for church membership, others who use the "You-can't-do-any-less-than-this-right-now" approach, and the "Ten-per-cent-is-the-minimum" people, have had their influence in certain quarters throughout Christendom. Many such have been used of the Lord, but the program described here will not satisfy these.

The church which teaches that the tithe is scriptural, and that there is no alternative in full dedication will be seriously aggra-vated by our approach.

Ours is a "Study-the-scriptures-and-see-what-Christ-says-to-you, start-somewhere-and-develop-as-the-Lord-leads" plan. For us the teaching of stewardship has long arms and steady hands.

REQUIREMENTS

It will be readily apparent that any teaching program on the stewardship of money must have either a minister or a strong lay leader who has deep personal convictions on this theme. If there is a combination of these two, the success of the work is much more certain.

In most churches today there are a few whose past experience in tithing would serve as a seedbed for raising up leaders of a serious training program. The wise pastor will be alert to discover these. He may also have at hand some person new in the faith who, by careful training, would become an excellent director of stewardship in the local church.

Some pastors have innocently fallen into habits of protecting their people from heavy demands. No minister would deny that there are attractive forces beckoning out there in the "Plain of Ono!" When Nehemiah was building the fallen wall of Jerusalem the scripture records,

Sanballat and Geshem sent unto me, saying, Come, let us meet together in some one of the villages in the plain of Ono. But they thought to do me mischief. And I sent messengers unto them, saying, I am doing a great work, so that I cannot come down: why should the work cease, whilst I leave it, and come down to you? (Neh. 6:2-3)

"Ono" may have been only a coincidental name, but it be-

41

comes a very real threat to the leader of any new movement. This is particularly true where pocketbooks are concerned.

A previous chapter describes the opposition which quickly came forward in our first presentation. This is to be expected. It may be a good thing. Planners with courage will seize the knives thrown their way to sharpen and shape a better program.

It is a fortunate leader who has some strong supporters who are thinking on the same wave length. Sometimes a minister must stand alone in what he believes to be a good thing. He will be criticized for this. Charges of "dictator" will be leveled in his direction but he will be ready to bear such accusations with the calm of Christ who, "when he was reviled, reviled not again."

Yet any minister soon learns that when he has one or several persons who will take the lead, it is much the better part of wisdom to let them do so. He must never leave any question as to his own position, but he does well, when possible, to support the leaders rather than lead himself.

When the conviction has shaped into a plan it must be carried to the official body of the church for their consideration. It would be well to make the presentation at one or several meetings prior to final decision. The particular plan presented will depend upon the conclusions reached by the committee. In our case, the plan of approach centered around the development of an official stewardship brochure. (See Appendix I for an example.) The plan originally introduced to the board included a brief outline of the steps in promoting the program as listed in this chapter. It then recommended that the official stewardship brochure be given to all new members who join the church and distributed to all members who had joined previous to the induction of the plan. After approval, this distribution was made by mail and

42

followed with a personal call at each home to explain and answer questions. The board should be frankly told that there will be dissatisfaction. The continual repetition required will elicit complaints. There may be people who will come as prospects and go elsewhere if they happen to select that Sunday of the pastor's stewardship sermon for their first look. The "All-they-do-is-talk-about-money" folks are a concern to any alert gathering of church officials. There are also numerous church members and potential church members who like to know how the attitudes of a particular church are shaped in this wise. They have belonged to congregations where there was no long-range plan. They have received little specific teaching on stewardship. The customary yearly budget drive and an occasional sermon on giving have left them as disorganized here as they may be in other areas. Some like it vague, but some do not, and for every one of our experience who has turned away, there are several others who have turned to a church which had a plan and spelled out frankly where it stood.

THE OFFICIAL STATEMENT

When a local board has voted to adopt a stewardship program it is well to have some written description for distribution to those interested. An attractive brochure which sets forth the purpose, the basic philosophy, and the plan of operation, is well worth its cost (see Appendix I). Ours is available at our office or on our literature table at certain times of the year. It is given to new members when they join and is on hand for anyone who wishes to study it. This defines a percentage giver, sets out the scriptural backing for proportionate giving, describes what we mean by a tithing church, and explains what the member can expect as he opens his soul to stewardship guidance within our framework. It is surprising how many of these are picked up and taken home or distributed in order to interest friends.

LEADERSHIP RESPONSIBILITY

One of the statements in our officer's procedure booklet reads:

All officers of this church shall promise to study and hold their hearts open to the practice of percentage giving.

Nominees for office in our congregation shall covenant to pray for and work in harmony with The Program Toward a Tithing Church herein described. Only those men who show an open mind toward percentage giving shall be nominated for a position on one of the boards of our church.

All officers of this church shall covenant to pray weekly for our stewardship program as per our officer's prayer covenant. All officers are expected to pray regularly concerning their own personal percentage giving.

This statement is discussed with all potential nominees by the church nominating committee. In our particular congregation no man is eligible for the church boards who has not completed our eight weeks' membership instruction course which is taught by the board officials during the regular church-school hour. In one of these lessons he is introduced to our philosophy of stewardship. The officer-nominee is also mindful of his "conversation responsibilities" in this connection. The brochure reads:

Officers may promote percentage giving by guiding discussions toward that theme. This can be done gracefully with care and prayer. Suggestions toward this end will be given at the annual school of instruction for church officers.

44

Steps in Promoting the Program

Paul's advice to "Hold fast the form of sound words" (II Tim. 1:13) is spelled out in a carefully controlled program of public presentations.

Our step-by-step development of the work is as follows:

Weekly

1. Each Sunday the church bulletin will carry a sentence thought-starter on the subject of percentage giving, such to appear under the by-line "Official Committee on Tithing." These sentence sermons are selected by the pastor and committee chairman. They are repeated at regular intervals throughout the year. (See Chapter VI.) These are omitted from the bulletin on Sundays when the pastor speaks on tithing or at such other times as the committee deems wise.

Monthly

2. Once each month percentage giving is to be mentioned from the pulpit. This is done in the announcement period or before the offering is received. It may take the form of a scriptural reference or some thought on percentage giving. (See Chapter VII for examples.) This should be done gracefully and officers are to see that it is kept in good taste. The pastor will welcome items to assist in this announcement. For example, clippings from newspapers are good. Here the minister may say, "One of our members handed me this interesting bit. I'd like to pass it on to you." Officers are urged to be alert to such "bits," particularly those with a human interest touch. Stewardship training can be interesting and attractive.

45

Quarterly

3. Once each quarter each department of the church school from the junior level up is to have a five-to-ten minute presentation on Christian giving. Literature selected by the committee is distributed to members of the church-school to conclude the talk. This material is planned with an eye to bringing attractive stewardship challenges into every home of the church, both prospect and member. These talks may be given by officers, committee members, or individuals who are asked to testify to their personal experience. Often in the adult classes outside speakers are brought in on these occasions to present a lesson of personal testimony.

Twice Yearly

4. Two times each year a letter goes from the official committee on tithing to the entire congregation. This letter will likely enclose a carefully selected pamphlet. It is the duty of the committee chairman to keep a library of such materials available to officers and leaders. These may be secured from many denominations and chosen at the discretion of the chairman and his committee. (See Appendix III.) On two Sundays of the year the pastor will deliver a stewardship sermon with emphasis on percentage giving. On these Sundays a well-chosen pamphlet may be enclosed with each worship bulletin.

Yearly

5. Once each year every organization in the church will have a brief presentation from some member of the committee on tithing. Handout pieces may again be used to climax this appearance. It is generally true that a five-to-ten-minute presentation with a dynamic punch will accomplish more than a longer dis-

course on this theme. Most classes and groups have other things planned on our stewardship emphasis day. Where organizations wish to give an entire program to the matter, it should be done attractively in an interesting manner.

Checkup

The committee chairman will keep a chart whereby he checks monthly, quarterly, semiannually and annually on the outlined program. It is his duty to remind the pastor monthly of mention from the pulpit. He also programs the presentations at departments and groups. He is to see that the congregational letter is sent, and he has general responsibility to spearhead the program.

V

Minor Matter of Major Importance

ONE DETAIL OF FIRST CONSEQUENCE IN THE INSTITUTION OF ANY
program of stewardship training is that *first pledge*. Unless this
is carefully planned and some system developed for its handling,
one of several things may happen:

1. The new member may not be canvassed after he becomes
affiliated with the church until the next annual budget drive.

2. If he is canvassed, it may be done abruptly in such a way
as to induce negative reactions.

3. He may delay pledging, or dally under various reasons,
until the officers in charge of new member pledges will either become discouraged or will seem insistent in an unattractive manner.

However accomplished, it is imperative in any properly
planned program for new member pledges to be secured quickly.
This is necessary, first, in order that the new member may have
some place to start in judging his own giving, secondly, that he
may be impressed with his Christian responsibility to give systematically in support of Kingdom's causes, and thirdly, in order

that the church may have some basis to judge the effectiveness of its official training.

The number one step in such a development is that the new member must be told in a positive and attractive manner what is expected of him. It is easy to "skirt" the subject by describing the church and all its benefits, by explaining the program in every area, and to say little or nothing about Christian giving because it may be embarrassing, or because it might be too demanding at the outset.

There are churches which have developed excellent methods, and any method which is good should be given serious consideration. Our system is described here, not because it is the last word, but because it is one way which secures almost one hundred percent results.

Our procedure is as follows: The pastor presents the new members with a copy of our brochure, "Program Toward a Tithing Church," upon the occasion of their uniting with the church. In some cases he has had the privilege of discussing our stewardship philosophy with those who become members. In others there has been no previous contact at this point. Our judgment is that the new members' first thoughts of Christian giving should be connected with spiritual responsibility. We believe this is best done by introducing the idea through the minister. Some of these people have belonged to other churches where very little was said specifically about giving. Others come from backgrounds where their first ideas automatically relate to things commercial. Therefore, the pastor gives them their pledge cards (both building and operating) and after clearly defining the church's philosophy of percentage giving, asks if there are any questions which the new members wish to ask. This meeting is held before the board of the church which helps lend an important atmosphere of solemnity.

It should be noted that this is only part of the first meeting with the new members. In our work, new members are received each Sunday. They come forward after the service to meet with the officers and are then taken to an appointed place where a church official explains four major facets of our church program: I. Our undershepherd program II. Our dollar-for-dollar benevolences III. Our instruction course IV. Our prayer program. He also distributes leaflets outlining what he has said.

During this period the new members fill out their membership blanks in preparation for the pastor's appearance. When he has finished greeting worshipers at the door, the minister then appears and is introduced by the vice-chairman. A typical pastor's talk to new members on any Sunday is as follows:

"We welcome you into our fellowship and are glad that you have come to build the Kingdom with us here. We trust that your new church home will be a blessing to you. We want you to know how you can be a blessing to it."

There are five duties of a church member. We are sure you will want to know what is expected of you. Suppose we liken these five duties to the five fingers on your hand.

1. *Study your church*. You have been told about our membership instruction course, and you will find this a very enlightening eight-week period. One of the books which is used in this course is [here the title of book is given—this is not a pamphlet but a full-length book] and we want you to have this as a home reference book and for your personal study. Many other helps are available in our church library and in the office. We believe strongly in an educated church.

2. *Regular attendance at worship* is the second duty which we will discuss. (Here follows appropriate discourse on good worship habits with a distribution of our Ten Rules for Worship card which we urge new members to place in a prominent place in their home or office.)

3. A third obligation of the Christian churchman is to *work in the church*. I have here your talent cards. These provide space for you to check both things you have done and things you would like to try. Please fill these cards out and have them ready for your undershepherd. They will be kept on file and recorded in our talent notebook. (Further selected statements are made relating to the stewardship of time.)

4. The fourth duty and privilege of the church member is *to practice the Christian stewardship of money*. Here are your pledge cards (Some churches prefer the word "commitment card," others "loyalty card." We use the term "pledge card" only because this is the preference of a majority of our officers. See Appendix II for copy of card wording.) which I will give you today and which you will consider carefully until your undershepherd makes his first call at your home. You will note that there are two cards here, one for the building fund and one for the general operating budget of the church. With these, we are giving you a lined envelope. Please place your cards in this envelope and seal it after you have filled them out. No one but the church treasurer will know what you give. This is a sacred matter in our church, not in order to protect us, but to put our pledges where they belong, as a covenant between ourselves and our Lord.

We also want you to know exactly what to expect and what the details are on our church's stewardship duties and plans.

For this reason I am giving you a copy of our official brochure.

Here you will read that this church believes in percentage giving. Our official attitude is, "We are not concerned with your share in our budget. What really matters is God's share of your income." We heartily recommend that you make a commitment to give a certain percentage of your income to God and grow in grace from that point. We recommend also your serious consideration of the tithe. We ask you to consider your pledge as a symbol of your commitment to Christ. We urge you to remain open to his guidance. Many of our members have found that percentage giving leads to a joyful new way of life. Your undershepherd will be glad to discuss this with you or one of the officers will come to your home at your invitation to answer any questions which you may have. (Note: Although it may seem that more time is given to this matter than to the other points, we carefully guard against this. The reader will observe that we have outlined point four, word for word, whereas other points are not described as fully in this book.)

5. Responsibility number five is *winning*. Somewhere in your circle of life there are those who do not know Christ or have no church affiliation. You become a member of the church today, but will you make this one reservation, "I am not all I should be as a member of this church until I have won at least one other person to my Lord." (Here our covenant of seventy, which is our evangelism work on the local level, is explained, and the member is told that he will be given a sheet describing this program in detail.)

When he has completed the "five fingers" description, the pastor asks if there are questions from those who are being received. If there are, which happens more often than might be expected, one of the board members is asked to answer. Then follows the asking of the questions which our denomination puts to new members and, following prayer, the members extend their greetings. The pastor in extending his hand of greeting gives the head of the family a packet containing the above-described material.

This period of reception lasts from thirty minutes to one hour and, although it may be inconvenient for both the officers and new members, those elected to office are asked to ready their schedules accordingly. Most people affiliating with us are already aware of this procedure through pulpit announcement.

In the opinion of our officers this plan is effective because it (a) indoctrinates the new member at once with the seriousness of his decision, (b) sets before him explicitly what is expected of him before he joins, (c) gives equal emphasis to each facet of his church activity, (d) leaves no question in his mind how his giving is to be handled, and (e) paves the way for those who are assigned to receive his pledge.

It may be of interest to note that there have been those who excused themselves from the group and did not join after hearing the explanation of what was expected. In some cases these have returned at a later date. Others have sought a church home elsewhere after further consultation with the pastor or with one of the officers. This happens infrequently and the vast majority of those coming into the church express genuine appreciation for what they have been told.

Next comes the actual securing of the pledge. No matter

how a church decides to do it, this is best done when it is done quickly.

Certain officers of the church may be assigned this responsibility either as a normal procedure for the denomination or by local custom. In our church, the undershepherd secures the pledge along with the talent cards.

This is not the occasion for a full description of our undershepherd plan. Briefly, we have developed our congregation in such a way that every member is prayed for daily by someone. This is the heart and purpose of our undershepherd program. Each undershepherd is given four families to form his "flock." In addition to daily prayer it is his responsibility four times a year to take our denominational devotional guide into each home in his flock. Otherwise he cares for their needs as his prayers direct.

When a new family unites with us, they are assigned to an undershepherd who contacts them immediately by phone and makes an appointment for his first visit. His wife may accompany him or he may go alone to this call. He presents the new members with their church membership certificate, gives them their quarterly devotional guide, discusses the church and answers questions, places emphasis on his daily prayer for each of them, asks them to keep him informed of their needs, tells them that he is responsible for their attendance at the membership instruction course, and picks up their talent cards and the sealed envelope with their pledge.

It may be argued that this program takes something away from the church board whose duty it is to "promote the grace of liberality." It is our judgment that this board has a much larger responsibility than merely picking up a pledge card. Their job

is to develop and carry out a program which will teach stewardship on a long-range basis. The undershepherd is asked to mention to his new flock member that he does this particular part
of his work for the official board in charge of church finance.

Undershepherds are appointed both from the officers of the
church and from non-officer male members. It is our experience
that the non-officers do the best job because this is their one responsibility, and because they have been selected especially to
the work.

It should be noted again that this is not the only good method
by which to accomplish the securing of that first pledge. It is
one effective method. The reader will be interested to note that
since we began using this procedure, 96 per cent of our new members have pledged within six weeks after their reception. Since
many of our men travel, delays are frequently caused by either
the undershepherd's or the new member's absence from the city.
But our records reveal that during the first six months of our cur-
rent year, forty-eight families have affiliated with us and at the
end of that period there were only two whose pledges were not
in. One was the case of a woman whose husband is seriously
ill, and the other resulted from temporary unemployment in the
home involved.

Our annual canvass is handled by the board who select and
train canvassers for this work. The undershepherd's only pledge
procurement is on the occasion of his initial call.

The importance of securing that first pledge immediately is
not only to establish stewardship responsibility for the new member, but it also has real value to the church. We are now given
some means of measuring the effectiveness of our stewardship

training. As previously cited, we do not excite ourselves at a low first pledge. But because we have this low pledge, as the years pass we are now able to judge how much of our training is breaking down old patterns and establishing the soul in healthy giving.

THE ANNUAL CANVASS

In addition to the "minor matter of major importance" involved in securing that first pledge, there must be some careful planning for an annual congregational approach to all members.

We use what is called "the pre-budget canvass." This development, which has revolutionized the giving of many congregations, involves three steps: (a) informing, (b) pledging, and (c) budgeting. It is apparent that this is the reverse of some procedures which make a budget; tell the congregation about it, and then secure pledges to underwrite it.

The major advantage of the pre-budget approach is that it sets the matter of church finance directly on the heart-altar of the individuals. With no budget to figure from, the member who wishes to be serious about his giving has no other place to go but to the Lord and his own conscience.

It will be obvious to the reader that this plan seems to be made for our program. After a full year's training, constant reminders through bulletins, talks, sermons, and literature, the pre-budget canvass is a natural for us. Such a canvass does not preclude careful planning and serious education—it requires these things! But when they have been attended with dispatch, the pre-budget canvass serves as the reaper to harvest the grown seeds.

Without saying so specifically, the pre-budget canvass implies: "God has called us together to build the Kingdom in this place.

How much creative activity for the Lord would you like your church to do this year?"

Our annual canvass consists of four training sessions for the canvassers. We have several principles which guide us here.

1. We believe in a large body of canvassers (they work two by two) with very limited contacts for each team. Usually we attempt to have enough canvassers on hand that no team need make more than two calls. This is not to save work, but to promote thorough contact with plenty of time given to each visit.

2. We believe in extensive training for our canvassers. Our four sessions are held during the church-school hour on Sunday morning. (Breakfast meetings on Sunday morning have been used.) These sessions center about:

Session I. An explanation and review of our official stewardship program. This is made by selected laymen and centers about personal commitment and percentage giving.

Session II. Two demonstration calls, staged carefully and rehearsed well. One call exhibits all the wrong approaches, the other presents the perfect call. These are a real riot and usually set the stage for much good will about the entire canvass.

Session III. Questions and answers from the canvassers directed to the leaders. This session clears the air of much misunderstanding and allows individuals to present new ideas which they have discovered.

Session IV— *Canvass Time*. Gathering of the canvassers on Sunday afternoon for assignment of cards and final instructions.

Two further items may be noted—all of our canvassers are directed to pray before entering the home. The use of the four-word prayer, "Lord, speak through me," is encouraged before ringing the doorbell and throughout the visit before answering questions.

Members of the church who are not canvassers are sent a postcard from the canvass chairman asking them to be home at certain hours on the particular Sabbath of the canvass. We receive no pledge cards at our church service and none are distributed prior to the calls. All canvassers are asked to sign their own cards and turn them in to the church treasurer before making any contacts. They have been told several times in the previous sessions that this will be expected.

While the canvassers are being trained, they and all non-canvassing members of the church are receiving weekly letters from the officials with an enclosure directing the thoughts of our people to their stewardship responsibilities. The number of these letters will vary depending on the committee in charge and the judgment of the church officials.

It is obvious also that the large gathering of canvassers accomplishes two things: a major number of family heads receive intensive training in session in addition to the correspondence contacts, and the number of canvass contacts is reduced in ratio to the number of canvassers trained.

CANVASSING THE NON-MEMBERS

In addition to contacting those who have joined our fellowship we have found it a rewarding experience to conduct a solicitation of parents who do not belong themselves but send their children to our church-school and their youth to our young peoples' activities. In this canvass we do not go into our official training program but frankly suggest that they will want to have a part in helping us finance the religious education of their loved ones. We tell them specifically in dollars and cents how much it costs us to keep each child in our church-school. This work is done by a specially trained group of canvassers. A letter precedes these calls, setting forth the figures and explaining the purpose of the forthcoming call.

We were happily surprised at the response. Not only did this canvass yield a sizable amount of money, but it caused the following interesting results: (1) Several families which had been sending their children began coming themselves and later joined the church. (2) Some parents of this group came to the church to talk over the matter which gave us an opportunity to discuss their own religious life. (3) Those who had been taking the church for granted were brought to reconsider their personal responsibility to the molders of their children's future.

VI

Statements for the Church Bulletin

EACH SUNDAY WE INCLUDE IN OUR WORSHIP BULLETIN A STEWARD-
ship paragraph signed by the official committee on tithing. In
most of these, the reader will observe some Scripture reference
which aims at turning the worshiper to God's word for personal
guidance.

The secretary who makes up the bulletin initials each insert in
her book as it is used. She rotates their use so that each is repeated
at proper intervals. She is free to use these, according to length
of statement as her space permits.

Since there are sixteen statements, if the entire set is used in
rotation, each paragraph will appear three times in one year. The
committee is invited to create new statements in keeping with
our theology and attitudes. Members of the congregation are
asked to assist in this training program. All entries are checked
by the committee and pastor before their use.

1. The Old Testament reveals that God, from the beginning of
   his contacts with men, instructed his followers to give one tenth
   of their income to him. (Lev. 27:30.) Those in the New Testament Church were directed to give proportionately as God

prospered them. (I Cor. 16:2.) This church invites its members to seriously consider percentage giving as a recognition that all life belongs to the Lord who gave his all for us.

THE OFFICIAL COMMITTEE ON TITHING

2. Money was the theme or in some way entered into the majority of the sermons and addresses of Jesus. One verse out of every six in Matthew, Mark, and Luke is on this subject. At least twelve of Jesus' thirty-eight parables deal with the right or wrong use of money. It is a prime matter to the Christian what Christ would have him do personally in the handling of his funds. This church urges all of its members to become percentage givers. We believe in starting at a specific point in our giving habits and letting Christ lead us on as we grow in grace. Read Matt. 22:37, Mark 12:30, and Luke 10:27. Then ask yourself, "Will my present giving habits lead to the full commitment which Jesus describes here?"

THE OFFICIAL COMMITTEE ON TITHING

3. Surely to give with the expectation that we will become rich for our own selfish purposes is blasphemous. Those who practice percentage giving and tithing witness, first, great spiritual blessing, and second, that all of life, including financial, social, personal, family, business, physical, mental—in short, the whole of life is blessed. God promised that those who give according to his guidance will know his abundance. (Mal. 3:10.) Jesus said that we will receive as we give. (Luke 6:38.) This Church urges its members to serious consideration of its giving habits for the good of the Kingdom and for the good of the soul.

THE OFFICIAL COMMITTEE ON TITHING

4. What do scholars of Christian truth have to say about tithing? Dr. Holmes Rolston in *Stewardship in the New Testament*

Church says, "The argument for the tithe moves in the realm of God's ownership and man's stewardship. It touches certain broad principles of religion which are common to all who believe in God. . . . But Christian giving must flow from our understanding of that which God has done for us in Jesus Christ. It is fair to say that with most Christians the will to tithe has been born of the surrender of the soul to the infinite love of God." This church believes in percentage giving as one more good starting place for growth in grace.

THE OFFICIAL COMMITTEE ON TITHING

5. God early promised joy as a reward of squaring our accounts with him. (Deut. 12:6-7.) Paul commanded his church at Philippi to rejoice in the Lord. (Phil. 4:4.) The inner radiance of Christian living can only be experienced when we are living as Christ directs our doing. Is your supply of Christian joy running low? Check your responses: Are you giving enough time to his service? Are you using your talents for his Kingdom? Is your stewardship of funds on a basis where he can lead you nearer to his will for you? This church recommends percentage giving as one more media by which we tie in to the joy of our Lord.

THE OFFICIAL COMMITTEE ON TITHING

6. It has been said that if any Christian tithes, he will have five surprises. He will be surprised: 1. At the amount of money he has for the Lord's work. 2. At the deepening of his spiritual life. 3. At the ease in meeting his own obligations. 4. At the preparation this gives to be a faithful and wise steward of the nine-tenths that remains. 5. At himself for not adopting the plan sooner. The church believes that its members must study the tithe as an ancient law of God; must recognize it as a spiritual blessing in many lives today; must consider their own giving in the light of the New Testament Christ who calls for total dedication;

and must start somewhere on a percentage giving program which symbolizes a definite response to the Lord who gave his all for us.

THE OFFICIAL COMMITTEE ON TITHING

7. Jesus said, "Where your treasure is, there will your heart be also" (Matt. 6:21). Where you spend your money does make a difference. It makes a difference in your outlook. It makes a difference in your insight. Perhaps you need to do something specific to improve your spiritual vision. This church recommends percentage giving as one more means of properly focusing all of life on the Lord who gives us all things. Have you made a covenant with God to give him a specific percentage of all that comes into your hands?

THE OFFICIAL COMMITTEE ON TITHING

8. What do scholars of Christian truth have to say about tithing? T. A. Kantonen in *A Theology for Christian Stewardship* says, "I am convinced that the tithers in our churches are by and large not Pharisees but humble and sincere Christians who have been led to use this ancient device as a helpful means for a steady expression of their gratitude and faithfulness to their Lord. . . . But I am also convinced that the true beginning of Christian stewardship is in a clean break with the false God mammon through complete self-surrender to the love of God in Christ." This church urges its members to percentage giving as a special symbol whereby we attest that Christ is the Lord of all our living.

THE OFFICIAL COMMITTEE ON TITHING

9. It is old, old; and though there are some who think it has been repealed entirely, the ancient follower of God never thought of changing its form. As a law, it was always the sacred tenth.

(Lev. 27:30.) The New Testament Church was directed to proportionate giving. (I Cor. 16:2.) For them, all life was a stewardship in response to the grace of God in Christ. This church urges its members to seriously consider tithing and percentage giving not as laws to be obeyed, but as symbols of response for what the Lord has done for us.

THE OFFICIAL COMMITTEE ON TITHING

10. The One who watched as the widow cast in her two mites, is also on hand today as his people bring their offering. As we read this story in Mark 12 or Luke 21 we note that the woman received Jesus' praise because she gave all that she had. There is no other fitting response to the love of God in Christ than total surrender of all we are and all we have. We recommend percentage giving as one more symbol that we know where our lives belong. Would your offering today be a fit subject for the eye of your Lord who gave his all for you?

THE OFFICIAL COMMITTEE ON TITHING

11. Question: Does the New Testament teach tithing? Answer: The New Testament teaches full response to the love of God in Christ. Jesus said that He came not to destroy the law but to fulfill it. (Matt. 5:17.)

We believe that New Tesetament teaching goes beyond the tithe to fulfill a higher law, this is the law of total commitment.

This church recommends percentage giving to its members as a starting place for financial growth in the Lord.

THE OFFICIAL COMMITTEE ON TITHING

12. It is not tithing which makes a person Christian. Percentage giving does not make you all you need to be as a follower of Christ. Let no one suppose that tithing and percentage giving are tests of one's Christianity. They are only the evidence of one's spir-

itual understanding, symbols of one's response to divine love, but they are acid tests of this. Are you serious about your commitments in practical ways? Read Eph. 5:1-2 this afternoon and ask yourself, "Does my pledge to the church and my giving to Kingdom's causes indicate a fit response to the Christ who gave himself for me?"

THE OFFICIAL COMMITTEE ON TITHING

13. Have you ever thought how your giving would change if Jesus stood before you waiting to receive your gifts? Would you give him exactly the same amount as you now give for God's work? Before you close your eyes tonight, ask yourself, "What would my Lord have me do about tithing?" Jesus, in reproving the proud Pharisees, gives them no credit for tithing. He says "These ought ye to have done." Does he mean that I must give one-tenth of my income to his church? There may be some question at this point but there is no argument here. Matt. 23:23 is a call for me to respond fully to divine grace. Am I doing all I *ought?*

THE OFFICIAL COMMITTEE ON TITHING

14. What do scholars of Christian truth have to say about tithing? As Christians we are interested in Jesus' attitude toward this ancient practice. Theodore H. Robinson in *Moffatt's New Testament Commentary* on Matt. 23:23 says, "The rabbis laid it down that everything that grew from the ground and might be eaten was subject to the law of the tithe, and a careful observer of the Law would carry this out to the last detail. Jesus does not condemn this practice—on the contrary he says, 'these latter ought you to have practised'—but he insists that men must not regard it as excusing them from more important duties." Our church believes that regular systematic giving is called for in New Testament living. We urge our members to set aside a definite

percent of their income, to covenant with the Lord for this, and to ask him to lead them on to total commitment.

THE OFFICIAL COMMITTEE ON TITHING

15. Some men obey the laws because they have been trained to obey. The Old Testament followers of God were educated in the tithe. The New Testament transcends to a higher plane as it calls us to obey the laws of the Lord as a response to his love for us. Most of us need specific starting places toward a fuller response. One of these is the call to percentage giving which our church issues to its members. We urge you to begin somewhere and grow in grace as God calls you on. We believe this program has scriptural backing in many places. One such is I Cor. 16:2. Ponder this verse and let Christ the Living Word speak to you through it.

THE OFFICIAL COMMITTEE ON TITHING

16. One of our tithers said, "Tithing is soul satisfying and it gives me the feeling that I am doing my part. I believe the Lord wants me to tithe. That is why I give ten per cent of all I receive to support his Kingdom." This church believes that every one of its members should study tithing seriously. We must recognize this practice as an ancient law which has brought rich blessing to multitudes of Christians and non-Christians. We also believe in the New Testament practice of starting somewhere and growing in grace. This is why we recommend percentage giving as a practical beginning to fuller following.

THE OFFICIAL COMMITTEE ON TITHING

VII

Sample Monthly Pulpit Statements

As A PART OF THE OFFICIAL STEWARDSHIP PROGRAM OF THE CHURCH, the pastor is obligated to give a call for percentage giving monthly from the pulpit. He is free to do this on any Sunday which he deems appropriate. This statement is usually made during the announcement period, before the offering, or prior to a hymn which might touch on the theme. We have found that it is well to guard against always giving it at the same time. For instance, if it repeatedly comes before the offering, there are some minds which will automatically deduce that percentage giving is only a tool for church finance.

The chairman of the official committee on tithing keeps a chart which he checks regularly to be sure that the program moves apace. If the first three Sundays of the month have passed without statement, it becomes the chairman's responsibility to remind the minister that his stewardship thought is due at the coming worship service.

The pastor welcomes suggestions from officers of the church. Those who find interesting items, or who have original thoughts on the theme, are urged to submit them for use.

Ordinarily the statements are limited to two or three minutes. They frequently point the worshiper to a consideration of some scripture verse which is in keeping with one of the major precepts: that each Christian must study God's word in order that Christ, the Living Word, may speak personally to him.

TWELVE SAMPLE PULPIT STATEMENTS

1. A Better Idea of God

Are you afraid of bankers? I was, until one day in Nebraska a bank president set me straight. He was an officer of our church and had the unusual ability to look deep into human hearts.

I had gone into the bank to borrow money. We were struggling to pay off some debts and a loan was important right now. I must have been very nervous for he suddenly said, "What're you so scared for? Didn't it ever occur to you that it's my business to lend this bank's money? If I know you're a good bet to pay it back, I like people like you coming in here."

So I explained to John how I had been embarrassed in my college days at a particular loan company. I admitted that my opinion of bankers was not good. I had the idea that they would all sit there sneering, hoping to make me ashamed. He did a fine thing for me that day when he said, "Relax boy! I'm your friend. This bank is real glad to help anyone who honestly tries to do right."

There is a verse in Isaiah (30:18) which is worth considering at this point. "And therefore will the Lord wait, that he may be gracious unto you." Your attitude toward God can make a mighty difference in your religion. If you think of him as a niggardly king who must be badgered to parcel out his goodness in small portions, that is one thing. If you think of him as Isaiah does here, that is something altogether different.

A friend of mine writes, "I have observed that God always blesses those who have shown him that they can be trusted." Some of us have made this discovery through the practice of percentage giving. It gives us a new idea of God. Rather than concentrate on how little we have, we begin focusing our minds on how much God has. Perhaps a more biblical approach to your funds is what you need to give you a thrilling new experience with the heavenly Father. The tithe is an ancient practice which is still a rich blessing to many of our people. The New Testament call is for total commitment of all we have. Percentage giving which puts aside a set percent regularly for Kingdom causes, can lead you to a fuller understanding of what God is really like. The Bible says, "And God is able to make all grace abound toward you; that ye, always having all sufficiency in all things, may abound to every good work" (II Cor. 9:8).

2. The Tenth Commandment

"Thou shalt not covet" has been called, "The forgotten commandment." Because it is tenth on the list it is sometimes treated with less importance than those which go before. In a recent discussion on the Ten Commandments one man quipped, "By the time I get to ten I'm already so embarrassed I want to close the book and go away."

Yet these four words carry with them one of the longest explanations in our biblical listing of the ten. In both Exodus (20:17) and Deuteronomy (5:21) where they are set out for the people, they are followed by many words to be sure that they are understood. In addition, "Thou shalt not covet" is repeated twice in the New Testament. We find it in Rom. 7:7 and Rom. 13:9.

To covet means to want things so much that we harm other people and harm ourselves to get them. Perhaps the desired item is something which will be all right for us someday, but we are not yet ready for it. It might be something which is right for others but was never intended for us.

The cause of coveting is man's failure to look to God for his supply. Phil. 4:19 says, "But my God shall supply all your need according to his riches in glory by Christ Jesus." Note the verse does not say that we will get all we want, but rather what we need. The person who trusts the Bible at this point will do his best, and having done that, he will know the joy of relying on the abundance of the Heavenly Father.

To covet is to believe that God's goodness will run out before it gets to us. To covet is to trust our own judgment rather than the wisdom of the Lord. He wants us to use our minds, our strength, our talents to their full capacity. But when we have done this, we can now wait for the fullness of his love to come into our lives.

In this church we recommend that all of our families become percentage givers. This means that a covenant is made with God for a definite portion of all that is received in that home.

One of the reasons why we are so enthusiastic about this way of stewardship is that it teaches us to trust God more. We do not worry now whether we are doing what we should. We have made a definite start at squaring our accounts with God and we accept the promise that he has what we need and that all our life is in his loving hands.

70

3. Vertical Giving

Bud H. was a great sprinter. He was a member of our college track team and our coach always said that he could have ranked with the best, except for one bad habit. He always ran with his head down! He put his chin on his chest, his eyes on the track, and dashed madly to many victories. But he often lost the big ones because his habit intensified with pressure. The tougher the race, the tighter he would lock his head downward and crash into the breeze.

Some of us live like that. Now and then we look up when the race slackens, but when the going is rough we glue our eyes to the things of this earth and drive madly on.

Seven words from Ps. 123:1 can make a mighty difference. You might write them on your heart and try living by them this week. Here they are: "Unto thee lift I up mine eyes."

A good place to begin checking our habits against that affirmation is in the Christian stewardship of our funds. Some of us, money-wise, live too much in the flats. We have reached a plateau and there is no upward thrust to our giving. It is possible here to run with our eyes down in such a way that we never get out of us the best that is in us. Vertical living is immeasurably aided by vertical giving.

This is another reason why our church believes in and preaches percentage giving. Those who follow this teaching discover one more practical way to lift up their lives to the Lord who is the divine source of life as it ought to be.

As you look at the cross above the communion table, notice that it would be a straight line if it were not for its vertical member. It will be worth while to note that a cross looks out of shape unless the "upward thrust" is the dominant factor.

These are seven great words for every phase of life at its best. "Unto thee lift I up mine eyes."

4. Action Brings Reaction

The golden-haired girl came into my study one day with a beautiful bowl of delicate flowers. They were of the midget variety which matched their mistress. She was only five, and her mother said that this was her idea. She wanted her pastor to share some of the loveliness from her own garden.

Being an adult, I said the wrong thing. "But are you sure you want to give me so many?" I asked. "Shouldn't you save some of them for yourself?"

"Oh no," she replied, "These are the kind that the more you pick, the more you have. Tomorrow there will be lots more."

It was a big lesson from a little lady. She had touched one of the great truths of the Lord.

Jesus said, "Give and it shall be given unto you" (Luke 6:38).

Paul put it this way, "He which soweth bountifully shall reap also bountifully" (II Cor. 9:6).

This is a mighty spiritual fact. It works for every area of life. If we hoard our ideas, we limit our usefulness. If we use them generously, more will be given us. If we build a tight wall about our lives, we always shut out more than we shut in. If we breathe shallow, we will have little room for fresh air in our lungs. Action brings reaction, and he who sends out love is sure to feel the love of God flowing back into his own heart.

We do not give in order to get, but getting is a natural result of giving, and the Bible repeats this theme often.

Maybe you're having a hard time because you have been holding on too tight to what God has given you. Our church recommends percentage giving because we believe the Scripture writers were "good men who were taught by the Holy Spirit." They set forth spiritual laws direct from God himself.

One rule which has blessed many people is the law of the tithe. It is still practiced by many Christians. Some have found it an excellent rule for money management and we urge your serious study of God's laws for your life.

5. It Doesn't Pay if It Doesn't Cost

There is an interesting story in II Sam. 24. David has been instructed to "Go up, rear an altar unto the Lord in the threshingfloor of Araunah the Jebusite."

So he goes. The farmer runs to meet his king, bows duly, and asks him why he should be seeking him.

David informs Araunah that he has come to buy his threshingfloor that he might build an altar. So the faithful owner, impressed with his ruler's selection of this site, waxes very generous. He not only offers to give the king the threshingfloor but tells him to help himself to the ox, the wood, and the necessary instruments. These will be a gift from Araunah to David. Then follows a classic reply. David says,

Nay; but I will surely buy it of thee at a price: neither will I offer burnt offerings unto the Lord my God of that which doth cost me nothing. So David bought the threshingfloor and the oxen for fifty shekels of silver.

This calls for some pensive pondering. How much is your offering to the Lord costing you? Do you hold to the high reasoning that unless it costs something it isn't worthy of your Lord? Is your financial stewardship of the token variety whereby you give casually in order to quiet your conscience or because it is expected that you do this?

Wherever did we get the puerile idea that Christians should make it as easy as possible? Certainly such a concept did not stem from the Master who said, "If any man will come after me, let him deny himself" (Matt. 16:24).

Our church unashamedly calls its members to a continual examination of their stewardship. We invite all of our families to begin somewhere, right now, to begin on a percentage basis with their church pledge and work toward higher percentages as God leads them. If your first reaction is, "But I can't afford that. I could never tithe." If that's how you feel, this may be good. Even tithing is not sufficient if it costs nothing for the tither.

Christianity is for the courageous. It is for those who give themselves to the Lord who gave his all. This is a startling truth: It doesn't pay if it doesn't cost. "I will not offer unto the Lord my God of that which doth cost me nothing."

6. The Fairness of God

In the parable of the talents there is an interesting observation. Jesus tells us that the man with five talents returned five talents to his Lord at the accounting. And the man with two talents brought other two talents to match what he had received.

But they both received the same promise. Matt. 25:21 is the Lord's award to the five-talent servant while Matt. 25:23 is his word to the two-talent worker. They both read, "Well done, thou good and faithful servant: thou hast been faithful over a few things, I will make thee ruler over many things: enter thou into the joy of thy Lord."

This identical remuneration to the nonidentical servants is a testimony to the fairness of God. It is true that some people have "more on the ball" than I have. It is also true that certain citizens have much more of this earth's good than others. But our King judges us both by whether we have rendered an honest return of what he has given us.

God's fairness is also attested in his scriptural rules for giving. In the Old Testament he instructs his followers to tithe. But in the New Testament he directs his people to give "as God hath prospered them."

There could scarcely be any fairer judgment of modern servants of Christ than this: "Did you do the best you could with what the Lord gave you?"

Our church believes that percentage giving will help you to bring your financial stewardship into line with what God wants from you. We urge you to set aside a definite percentage of your income, covenant with the Lord to give this regularly, and let Christ lead you to that day when you can hear him saying, "Well done, thou good and faithful servant."

7. Unbaptized Pocketbooks

One of our officers handed me an amusing story. I thought you might like it.

According to this tale a certain person was baptizing one of his new converts in a creek. But as he approached his preacher, the neophyte suddenly remembered something. "Just a minute," he said as he ran back out of the water, "I forgot to give my billfold to my wife."

"Come on back here," shouted the man of the cloth in a voice for all to hear, "I've already got too many unbaptized pocketbooks among my people."

Prov. 3:6 says, "In all thy ways acknowledge him, and he shall direct thy paths." It is possible for us to be very basic in our theology; to accept most of the doctrines of the church; to be obnoxious about certain rules of Christian living; to have a zeal for evangelizing the unchurched; to know the Bible from cover to cover; and at the same time to close our minds to God's teaching on the Christian stewardship of our money.

Jesus must have been a nuisance to those who didn't like hearing the divine demands on their money. One verse of every six in Matthew, Mark, and Luke deals specifically with a man and his possessions. Nearly one third of those marvelous parables which Christ told focus on this theme.

Whenever you find yourself squirming at the mention of how much God expects of your income, it is highly probable that the trouble is not what you hear but deep in your own heart.

This church commends the practice of percentage giving which sets aside a definite percentage for God's work and moves on as he calls. We believe this is the scriptural way to live. When you were baptized into the Christian Church did your pocketbook go with your commitment?

8. Poverty Complex vs. God's Love

An old lady taught me a real lesson. She was a devout grandmother in the wee town where I worked one year and I would sit long at her feet for lessons in right living.

One day when I was particularly worried lest I not have enough to finance a vital matter with me, she sensed that I was troubled. She had a knack for probing the depths and before I knew it, I was pouring out my heart to her.

When I had explained how I must have a certain amount of money if I were to go back to school she asked, "Are you doing the best you can?" "Yes," I replied, "I'm working hard, saving my money, and I honestly think I'm doing my best."

"Son," she replied, "when you are doing your best, don't ever think your little needs are beyond God's ability to supply."

The Bible says, "My soul, wait thou only upon God: for my expectation is from him" (Ps. 62:5). I learned from that little old lady, and from many saints since, that one of life's basic secrets is to do one's best and then wait expectantly for God. Whenever things are not going well, I am apt to find that I have been looking elsewhere than to the Lord who knows what I need and is ever ready to provide for me if I have done my best.

There is a psychological term for extreme cases of low expectancy. It is called "the poverty complex." Many people I know are afraid that life's goodness will run out. They tremble lest there may come a big depression in their personal affairs.

God expects us to plan well and to manage our affairs with the good sense he has provided us. But we put a hobble to our soul when we concentrate on life's lack rather than God's love.

One way we can prevent this is by living as the Scripture directs us. God early set forth the rule of tithing for those who would know him fully. Our church recommends serious attention to this Old Testament law. We also encourage the New Testament practice of proportionate giving. We urge you to set aside a definite percentage of your income, to give this first and give it regularly, and by this means to keep your soul exposed to the holy pull of full commitment. We know that those who will proceed in faith will one day experience the thrill of the Psalmist's words, "My soul, wait thou only upon God; for my expectation is from Him."

9. Heavenly Cadence

Any way we figure it, at least three dozen times the Old Testament says that man's tithes belong to God. This word in Lev. 27:30 is repeated again and again: "The tithe . . . is holy unto the Lord."

The Hebrews assigned symbolic values to numbers and ten for them signified increase. It is still true in our day that with each count of ten we begin a new series. Ten, twenty, thirty, forty are familiar sounds to any teacher of basic arithmetic.

Much of life moves in specific cadence. Every snowflake is different from every other snowflake, but each has the six point pattern. Certain flowers always have the same number of petals. These and other voices of nature attest to God's harmony in the universe.

When a voice is "off" in the choir we say, "He is not in harmony," and the symphony conductor may say to his violinist, "You are playing out of tune."

As new discoveries are made in every realm we uncover more of the eternal rhythm at the heart of God's world. Some things are for sure and when we go against these certainties we find that life is not as it should be.

The wise Creator of men and things did not leave men to guess how they should give. In the Old Testament he called for "tithes and offerings." In the New Testament, through the apostle Paul, he instructed his followers to give "as God hath prospered."

This church teaches percentage giving, serious study of the tithe, and continual progress toward full commitment. We recommend that every family in our membership give serious consideration to heaven's claim on its earthly goods. That is why we encourage you to give up the practice of giving so much per week, or this much each year. We urge you to covenant between God and yourself that you will return a set percentage to him regularly. The reason for our existence is to live in full harmony with the Lord.

10. One Hundred Per Cent for God

This church has many members who tithe. We recommend that every member of our congregation give serious consideration to percentage giving. We urge our people to start somewhere, regularly setting aside a definite covenanted portion of their income.

But let no one suppose that this is a matter of giving God his share. It is true that the Bible says, "The tithe is the Lord's." But the same Holy Rule of life makes it clear that all we have belongs to the heavenly Father.

Moffatt translates Gen. 28:22 like this: "I will give thee faithfully a tenth of all that thou givest me."

This is Jacob making a vow out of a vital spiritual experience. Whether he thought of it like this or did not, we find him here touching on a mighty truth. Everything we receive and all that we are is the result of God's grace operating in our direction.

In all of our teaching on Christian stewardship, in our discussions with other people, and in our prayers that we may live our lives as the Bible teaches, we must recognize this fact. When we put our giving on a percentage basis, it is not because this much of our income is God's money. Rather, it is all his. Our time, our work, our health, our service, our words, our minds, and our very selves, belong to the Lord. He gave them to us and he can take them from us at his call. Our pledges are only a token that every bit of everything we have is from him.

Let all of our stewardship be in the spirit of Jacob's words, "I will give thee faithfully a tenth of all that thou givest me."

11. Mrs. Smitjers Little Brown Crock

In one church where I was pastor there was a little old lady who lived in a tiny home several miles out in the country. I called on her regularly, not out of pastoral duty, but because she always blessed me with her unfailing faith and constant good cheer.

Life had been hard for Mrs. Smitjers if you judged her by worldly measures. But she never knew bitterness, and her head was unbowed, because she lived all her life by heavenly standards.

Her Bible was well-worn, much marked, and she practiced what she read there. One of the Old Testament teachings which she applied religiously was the practice of tithing. Mrs. Smitjers kept a little brown honey-crock high up on the topmost shelf of her kitchen. Always before I left, she would take her stool, climb the steps carefully, and reach far back into the cupboard to get the pennies and nickels she had been putting aside for the Lord. She would say proudly with a twinkle in her one good eye (she had lost the other in a girlhood accident), "You can tell how much I earned, pastor, by how much there is here. Since you called last time, I've been putting in my tithes and it's all right here."

Mrs. Smitjers supported herself by selling milk from her goats, honey from her bees, and eggs from her hens to a sizable number of neighbors and friends.

When it came time for "a wee word from the Book" and our prayer together she would say, "Read me a bit from the Thirty-seventh Psalm." Always she wanted me to include this one verse, and when I came to it she would smile out of her wrinkled face and muse, "I love that, pastor. Ain't that just beautiful?" Here is the verse: "I have been young, and now am old; yet have I not seen the righteous forsaken, nor his seed begging bread."

It is a thrilling experience to let oneself go on the everlasting arms. We can know this joy and sense this soul-quieting trust when we know that we are living life by God's direction.

This is one more reason why our church urges all of its members to practice percentage giving and move always toward full surrender of life to Christ. God does not promise us a million dollars if we do this, but over and over he does pledge that if we live his way we will know the warm glow of divine companionship throughout all our years.

12. *A Delightsome Land* (Suggested for a patriotic season)

In the last book of the Old Testament there is a verse which reads: "And all nations shall call you blessed: for ye shall be a delightsome land, saith the Lord of hosts."

Immediately, any good citizen tunes in to a promise like that. If I were to ask, "Would you like to help produce a delightsome land which all nations would call blessed?" there is hardly a person who wouldn't respond. This is as it should be. The Bible tells us that we have a real obligation to the civil authority under which we live. As Christians we are anxious to fulfill our responsibilities to our government.

Two verses prior to this promise of national blessing, the prophet describes how this can come about. It says here:

Bring ye all the tithes into the storehouse, that there may be meat in mine house, and prove me now herewith, saith the Lord of hosts, if I will not open you the windows of heaven, and pour you out a blessing, that there shall not be room enough to receive it.

This famous tithing word from Mal. 3:10 is often interpreted on the basis of individual rewards for those who will accept God's challenge. But we should also give serious thought to this larger promise. Our Christian stewardship does have mightier connotations than our own little lives. We can become better citizens of our nation when we become better citizens of God's kingdom. Always, we bless our country when we obey the laws of the Lord.

This church emphasizes percentage giving. We believe that it is good for a family to make a covenant with God to give a definite portion of their income. We invite each unit of the Lord's people to grow in grace from this point as Christ leads. We believe in doing this as a symbol of our first loyalty. We believe that we have a real obligation to the flag under which we live. But we also know that the finest thing we can do for our country is to recognize that our first citizenship is with the kingdom of God.

Only when we are living the Lord's way will we experience this reality: "All nations shall call you blessed; for ye shall be a delightsome land, saith the Lord of hosts."

VIII

Starter Ideas for Tithing Talks
to Children and Youth

As PREVIOUSLY DESCRIBED, ONE REGULAR FEATURE OF OUR PROGRAM
Toward a Tithing Church is the quarterly presentation in each
church-school department. This is always done by a layman,
either some member of the official committee or a carefully
chosen non-officer. In most congregations there are men and
women who, if invited, will take to this work with enthusiasm.

We have found that an object-lesson approach is the most successful. This is particularly true in the children's departments,
but when properly done may be equally effective with adults.
People who are asked in advance to be the speakers for the
year, will be on the lookout for useful ideas.

Usually, a pamphlet of the committee's choosing is distributed
at the end of the talk. This serves several purposes, not the least
of which is to carry the stewardship claims of Christ into homes
which may not be regular in their worship habits. It also makes
a good medium for delivering the message to prospects. We do
not include our prospective-member list in mailings of the bian-

nual tithing letter. Neither does this list receive our national magazine nor our state denominational paper; therefore, we are glad to have some religious matter delivered in this way.

Investigation in specific cases reveals that children are likely to explain to their parents what they learn from an object talk. These people often are not acquainted with such thoughts. Frequently when our callers visit at these homes, people ask questions concerning our official stewardship policy. This creates an added opportunity for teaching.

It is our experience that brief and incisive talks on this subject will do the most to create interest and stimulate later thinking.

It is wise to co-ordinate these talks when several speakers are used. This saves embarrassing repetition, particularly of object sermons.

Here are four starters which have met with enthusiastic response.

1. THE HUGE POCKET

(Object needed: A robe with generous folds)

One day Jesus said to his followers, "Give, and it shall be given unto you; good measure, pressed down, and shaken together, and running over, shall men give into your bosom. For with the same measure that ye mete withal it shall be measured to you again" (Luke 6:38).

In our Lord's day money was not always the medium of exchange. This meant that if you were selling something at the market you might receive several bushels of grain in exchange for your product.

You realize that it would make a big difference whether the person who was paying you gave you a pressed-down basketful or tried to fluff it up so you wouldn't get full measure. When the grain was shaken togther and pressed down, or if the basket were filled until it ran over, you could be sure you were receiving full value.

This may be what Jesus meant when he gave us this verse.

But you will remember that the words of Luke also included the phrase, "into your bosom."

Some Bible teachers say that this has an interesting meaning. When you made an "into your bosom" deal, it meant that you could pick up the bottom of your robe like this and make a huge pocket up against your heart. Then the person who was paying you would pour his goods into this big space until you couldn't hold any more or until it was full. This phrase came to mean the most generous kind of giving.

Jesus always taught that we get in the same ratio that we give. If we shortchange people, life has a way of doing the same to us. If we practice sending out love and good will, we experience the joy of "into our bosom" measurements coming our way.

There are laws of God which are written into the universe. One of these is the law of God's response to our opening. This law indicates that the Father's love comes into our hearts as we open our hearts to receive it.

The purpose of the Christian Church is to get men to respond to the love of God in Christ. We believe in doing everything we can to fill our souls with his redeeming light.

This is one of the reasons why our church teaches percentage giving. This is not in order to finance a budget. It is rather so that our people might do something definite now about their giving, and grow steadily in grace, as a symbol of their response to God's love.

(Here follow words on our official motto. If there is time, questions and answers may be helpful.)

2. IVORY

(Objects needed: A box of Ivory Flakes and a bar of Ivory Soap.)

How many of you know what color ivory is? (Here let the children respond.)

Ivory is almost always associated in our minds with something white. It stands for purity in religious writings and the dictionary says that purity is: "freedom from dirt—cleanness, moral cleanness."

There is a right way and a wrong way to do everything. This is also true of our giving.

Today I want to tell you how Ivory Soap and Ivory Flakes were named. Once there was a man named Harley Proctor. He was one of the founders of the famous Proctor and Gamble soap company. He lived in Cincinnati, Ohio, during the days of the Civil War.

One day a worker in his factory allowed the soap-mixing machine to run too long. This machine, which was called a "crutcher," beat this particular batch of soap so long that it was much lighter than usual. When it was made into bars and cakes, the soap floated. Someone else suggested that it be reboiled but another man said, "Maybe people will like it." They did, and customers who were used to fishing at the bottom of the tub for their soap bought the new product and were glad to have it.

For a while this soap was marketed without a name. Nobody could think of a good title for it. Then one Sunday, Harley Proctor heard a hymn at his church which gave him the name he had been wanting. The gospel song which he heard was "Out of the Ivory Palaces." It is a hymn which tells about the pure white mansions in heaven. Mr. Proctor decided that "Ivory" would be a good word for his new product and that's how Ivory Soap and Ivory Flakes were named.

Mr. Proctor was a devout man who believed in being very careful about his stewardship of money. Mr. Proctor was a tither. This means that he set aside ten cents out of every dollar which he earned. This was his pledge to his church.

There are many people in our church who live by this rule. They have studied the Bible and believe that God wants them to do this. In the Old Testament it was a law which everyone followed. When Jesus came, he said that *all* we have belongs to the Lord. The apostle Paul instructed his church at Corinth to set aside regular offerings as God had prospered them.

In our church we teach percentage giving. This is the business of promising the Lord we will give to his church a definite percentage of everything we receive. We do this as a sacred symbol of our recognition that all we have belongs to Christ.

(Here follow personal words on our church's official motto. If time permits questions and answers may be helpful.)

3. You Can't Outscoop God

(Objects needed: A teaspoon and a toy shovel, or a toy shovel and a real shovel.)

Thomas Johnston worked as a janitor in a church where our pastor was the minister. He also preached in a small church each Sunday.

One day he gave our minister an interesting philosophy of

Christian stewardship. When they were discussing giving, Thomas said:

You can't outscoop God. I have observed that if I dish it out with a spoon, that's how I gets it back. But if I dishes it out with a shovel, it always comes back to me big. The fact is that the Lord may even do me better. Sometimes when I put out with my spoon, God gives me back by the shovel full, whereas if I gets real generous and uses my shovel, God uses a great big bull-dozer to give back to me. No sir, you can't outshovel the Lord. He always does you as good as you do him or he does you better. I tries to get my people to see that if you don't give nothin' you ain't likely to get nothin' much in return. But when you really opens up, the good Lord is sure to open up to you. This is a holy rule and it can't ever be beat.

In his homely way, Thomas is teaching what the Bible teaches.

(Here follow selected Scripture verses from the Old and New Testaments which indicate the rule of reaping as we sow.

The speaker will carefully choose his words to carry the message that percentage giving is one more way by which we align our lives with the channels of God's grace. Those who speak to children and immature Christians will want to carefully plan their approach when using such ideas as these. The correct theme is: We do not give systematically in order to get what we want! We give systematically in order to get in line with what Christ wants for us!)

4. Tithin' Eggs!

(Objects needed: Nine average-size eggs and one large one, or a sign with wording below.)

Once there was a lady who put a sign up by her farmhouse which read:

| Hen eggs | 35 cents a dozen |
| Tithin' eggs | 45 cents a dozen |

Travelers were often curious about the sign so they stopped to buy from the woman. When they asked her to explain, she would bring out two baskets of eggs. She would point to one basket and say, "These are hen eggs." Then she pointed to the other basket and announced, "These are tithin' eggs."

"See the difference?" she would ask, "the tithin' eggs are larger. I have been tithing to my church for a long time. Every day when I gather the eggs in, I place them in groups of ten. Then I pick the largest egg from each group and put it in my tithin' basket. I sell these for the extra price so that I'm not only tithing my income but I'm making some extra money for my Lord."

The Bible talks often about tithes and offerings. This means that the people were supposed to bring ten percent of all they received as their tithe. In addition they were to give something extra as their offering. The egg lady was living by an ancient rule which was law in the Old Testament. The same law is practiced by thousands of Christians today and by many people in our church.

Jesus had a bigger law. He said that everything we have belongs to God and we should let him have all of ourselves. As a symbol of this recognition, many other persons in our church practice percentage giving. This means that they set aside a definite percent of all they receive for their pledges to the church. This is a good way to begin a specific program of personal dedication of funds.

(Here follow words on the official slogan of our church.)

IX

Sample Congregational Letters

EACH YEAR THERE ARE TWO OFFICIAL LETTERS FROM THE COMMITTEE
on tithing to all members of the church. The following points
are noteworthy:

1. We find that the most effective mailing in this work is
one which quotes from members of the church. In the second
letter presented here members of the church are relating their
own experiences. Names are not used with these quotes.

2. A suitable pamphlet or handpiece is enclosed with each
semiannual letter.

3. It is well to concentrate the letter on one idea. For example
in the first letter cited the major concept is: "Tithing is a practical means of relating our lives to God."

4. We find it best to have the letters signed by persons rather
than the abstract signature, "Official Committee on Tithing."
This makes the letter personal, friendly, and specific for those
who may wish to follow it up by further contact.

LETTER #1

Dear Fellow Member:

Every Christian knows that the more he centers his life on God, the
better things go for him.

This is the big reason behind the official stewardship program in our church. We are doing all we can to get as many people as possible on a percentage giving basis. This means that our members are asked to covenant with God for a set percent of their income. After starting somewhere on this spiritual ladder each family is urged to grow in grace as Christ leads them on.

Percentage giving and tithing are practical reminders of the Lord who gave his all, and who still gives us all.

Often the Bible promises that right giving leads to God's increased presence in our lives. Prov. 11:25 pledges, "He that watereth shall be watered also himself." Isa. 58:10 puts it, "If thou draw out thy soul to the hungry, and satisfy the afflicted soul; then shall thy light rise in obscurity, and thy darkness be as the noon day." The New Testament says, "To do good and to communicate forget not: for with such sacrifices God is well pleased" (Heb. 13:16).

All of our church's teaching on the subject of giving is for one purpose above all others—*that we might know the Lord better.*

Toward that end, we who were elected to guide the affairs of our beloved church, urge your serious consideration to every word of our official teaching on stewardship.

Faithfully your friends,

The Official Committee on Tithing (Names of officials follow)

LETTER #2

Dear Church Member:

For some time now we have been talking about percentage giving and tithing in our church. We thought it would be interesting to get the reactions of a few who have tried it. Here is what they say:

A housewife: "Percentage giving makes for a happier partnership with God. It gives the individual a broader, deeper feeling of fairness and security. It works for a most satisfying sense of values."

A chemist: "When you tithe because you feel that God wants you to tithe, you have the happy feeling which only comes from doing God's will."

A tax executive: "I believe the Lord prospers, in one way or another, those who tithe. I believe that if members start to tithe they will enjoy it, will feel better about their church life, and will always continue to tithe."

A popular teacher: "Jesus teaches us that a man's attitude toward God is revealed by his attitude toward his property. I find that he was right. Since becoming a percentage giver I have a greater respect for property of every kind. Also when I have made out my check for the promised percentage to my Lord, I find greater satisfaction in using the remainder."

A clerk: "When I first heard this business of 'God's share of your income' and all that talk about tithing, it made me furious. I thought, 'This is all right for rich folks, but not for me.' But gradually the idea took hold and I wouldn't go back to my old way of living for anything. In addition to the honest feeling I get from it, I couldn't begin to tell you how much fun I have had watching what went out and what came in since I took God at his word."

By now you have noticed the zest and joy which these fellow members have experienced. We cherish this experience for every family in our church. We heartily recommend that you join the growing number of percentage givers and tithers in our congregation.

Sincerely your friends,

The Official Committee on Tithing (Names follow)

X

Suggested Sermon Thoughts

TWICE EACH YEAR IN THE PROGRAM OUTLINED, THE PASTOR DELIVERS a sermon on stewardship with an emphasis on percentage giving or tithing. The first of these is usually given in May or June and the second in October before the annual budget canvass. Usually, the fall presentation is made prior to pledge Sunday and is designed to present teaching on the general theme rather than to relate specifically to the canvass.

The official teaching of the church is repeated, not only because repetition is a part of good education, but in order to reach new members who have joined since the last such sermon, those who missed the prior stewardship Sunday, and those whose minds may have been previously closed to the subject.

The two sermons which follow focus on (1) The urgency of following Christ all the way and (2) The practice of giving to God *first* as the right way to conduct all life's affairs.

SERMON I

A HOLY OUGHT?

Text: "These ought ye to have done" (Matt. 23:23).

A DIGNIFIED GRAY-HAIRED GENTLEMAN CALLED ONE SUNDAY ON A young pastor and his wife. They were in their second church out of seminary and their visitor represented an influential church in a prosperous Midwest city. He called to see if the youthful minister might be interested in moving to this prominent pulpit.

They took him to dinner and had a fine visit. The interesting guest described the proposed move. He related the numerous advantages which his church offered. He told of their program and outlined the beauties of their town. But he stumbled somewhat when the pastor's wife asked him to describe the minister who had recently left the proposed pulpit. Here the handsome visitor sat back, smiled graciously, and said, "I think the finest thing I could say about Dr. M. was that he never embarrassed anyone."

Jesus was not like that. Sometimes his followers must have blushed bright red.

In our scripture setting today, Jesus is addressing the most influential people of his day. When we put our ear down to the gospels, we can hear deep rumblings in the crowd as he says: "Woe unto you, scribes and Pharisees, hypocrites! for ye make clean the outside of the cup and of the platter, but within they are full of extortion and excess."

We are tempted now to go away and pretend we never knew him. Sometimes Jesus was, and is, so very embarrassing. An anonymous wit has said, "Religion is not alone for the purpose of comforting the afflicted. It is also for afflicting the comfortable." By this standard Jesus knew his business. He is the King of Love and Shepherd of souls, but he is also a mighty needler.

Some of us would be afflicted if we would take an honest look at our stewardship of time and life and money. There is a jarring statement in the passage of scripture from which we have quoted. We find these words in both Matthew and Luke. The phrase is: "These ought ye to have done."

The verse in its entirety reads: "Woe unto you, scribes and Pharisees, hypocrites! for ye pay tithe of mint and anise and cummin, and have omitted the weightier matters of the law, judgment, mercy, and faith: these ought ye to have done, and *not* to leave the other undone."

There are scholars who insist that these words are a gloss, that is, an addition to the original words. Therefore, they argue it is not right to say that Jesus is here contending for the tithe.

There is another school of Bible students who insist that Jesus' word "ought" refers back to "judgment, mercy and faith" rather than to "the tithe" of small things.

Still another group says that Jesus is neither condemning the tithing of these Pharisees, nor commending it. Therefore, say these, this passage represents neutral ground in the mind of our Lord.

But when the discussion has died away, some of us are left with a definite feeling that such arguments are inconclusive. What if Christ meant that the tithe was not only right but the expected thing from serious servants of God? One of the commentaries says, "There is no need for one set of duties to jostle out another: but of the greater our Lord says 'Ye ought to have done' them; of the lesser, only 'Ye ought not to have left them undone.'"

The "mint, anise and cummin" to which this passage refers were the smallest things which Christ could have used for illustration in a world without microscopes. We must remember that Jesus had been raised in the synagogues. Did he accept the tithe of everything as natural and right?

The proper approach for us is to study these words and let our Lord as the Living Word speak personally to our own hearts.

When we refuse to ignore this passage as unimportant to our guidance, we find that the master teacher used the word "ought" only three times as a directive. Once he told the disciples that they ought to be humble; he said it as he washed their feet. On another occasion he counseled, "Men ought always to pray." Our text today is Christ's third use of the word.

The dictionary describes "ought" with these words: "to be bound . . . to be necessary . . . to require." Webster says that "ought" is the same word as "owe."

When we listen long to these words of Jesus, we sense a note of warning. Tithing can be dangerous if it is not properly motivated. The Pharisees apparently expected that their tithing, and their other scrupulous following of the law, would qualify them for divine approval. They seem poised as Jesus begins to speak, ready for his accolades. They had been praised for their goodness so often that they must have fully anticipated another word of congratulation. By their payment of one tenth of their garden seeds they waited to be heralded as the perfect examples.

It must have been a terrific jolt to their egos when our Lord crashed in on them. We should note that he was not scolding them for tithing. He was condemning them, rather, because they were so proud of the fact that they were doing it. He was hitting directly at their tendency to *do* their religion rather than *be* their religion.

It was embarrassing because this strange rabbi revealed that their giving did not go deeper than their pocketbooks. They tithed to store up credit with God. But they had forgotten this— *Life is not for God to honor us! It is for us to honor him and all of our living should be to that end.*

If everyone in this congregation were a tither, do you think Jesus would tell us what good little Christians we are? Wouldn't he be more likely to say that because we live in a great land, in a lovely city, in beautiful homes, in pleasant surroundings—because of these, our responsibility is even greater? He might be glad that we tithe, but he would not burst with pride at our doing so. It is much more likely that he would go deeper to see if we were Christ-centered at the core.

As we sit in stained-glass splendor let us continually examine our reasons and our motives. We do not serve, nor build, nor labor, nor give for some heavenly medal of honor. We do these things from a sense of holy compunction if we do them Christ's way. This which we do should be from the natural overflow of deep communion with the Christ who said, "These ought ye to have done."

But these words have another meaning. It is true that Jesus believed in the law of the tithe. Yet he also gave men another law which proves itself to those who will dare to live by it. This is the law of abundant returns for those who give for right reasons. In one of his most famous sayings Jesus stated: "Seek ye first the kingdom of God, and his righteousness; and all these things shall be added unto you" (Matt. 6:33).

Constantly our Lord asserted that those who would center their

97

souls on God would find his love apparent in every area of their lives.

It is wrong to tithe if we do it in order to be honored, or to be prospered, or for any selfish reason. But if we tithe out of love for God, his love will be a real and vital part of our existence.

Are you afraid that if you were to give more it would tear up your budget and there wouldn't be enough left to pay the bills? Do you think that the Lord of perfect love would tell you that you ought to do something which would be harmful?

Is it possible that Christ said, "These ought ye to have done," because he knew that if we did it out of pure commitment it would richly bless us? He loves us. He wants us to experience the warm glow of his full presence. His directives are for that reason also.

He knew that our thoughts are like trains which run out to the supply yards to bring back what they are sent for. Our attitudes are the orders carried to the storehouse manager. If we are forever sending out little trains traveling by fear orders, we will get back trains loaded with fear thoughts. When we send out trains of trust, loaded with thoughts of high expectancy, we may be surprised at the abundant love which God sends back. Jesus said that no matter what our need, God is able to supply it. He wants us to have the fullness of our heavenly Father's goodness. Might this be one more reason for a "holy ought"?

This church does not insist that its members tithe. That would be untrue to our tradition whereby each person, having accepted Christ as his Lord and Saviour, is urged to study the Scriptures and let the Holy Spirit speak to his own soul.

But let there never be any misunderstanding of our official position on the stewardship of our possessions. Our motto is: "We are not concerned with your share of our budget. What matters is God's share of your income." We urge our members to start today on a percentage giving basis. We invite all of our families to covenant with the Lord to give a definite portion of all that comes into their hands. This is not in order to return to God something because he has been nice to us, but rather a symbol of our recognition that all we have is his. We feel a holy urgency about this because it relates us practically to the Lord in a specific way, and it gives us a definite starting point from which to grow in grace.

It is always well for us to remember that the joy of Christian commitment is not a quasi-joy rubbed in from the outside. If you have said, "I can't tithe. We are doing all we possibly can already. I think this is the most impossible thing I ever heard. This must be the 'mad preacher' Paul mentioned; those officers are insane; that church has lost its mind to think it can sell me on an idea like that!" If you have said these things, this may be good. It indicates that you have been thinking and perhaps hurting.

That's part of Christianity too. Through his resurrection, Jesus is alive today and ready to help each one of us live victoriously every moment of Monday, Tuesday, Wednesday, and every hour of every day.

But the Christian experience centers also in the cross. Perhaps your stewardship needs the cross. Christianity is never Christianity without the agonizing, wrenching pain that tears away sin and selfishness.

Life with the Lord is beautiful, but it isn't easy. It never was easy. Some things must go before Christ can walk with us. We must not dismiss this matter lightly until we turn our eyes to Calvary and view there the one who gave his all for us.

We can know the tremendous life which comes when Jesus really takes over the soul. But we can only know it when we understand that Christianity is not for nice people who give to be praised, or give to get, or give for any other reason than this: *Christ is the answer! He calls for heroes! His commands are holy orders! We dare not listen lightly whenever we hear him say, "These ought ye to have done."*

Sermon II
Make Me a Little Cake First

And the word of the Lord came unto him, saying, Arise, get thee to Zarephath, which belongeth to Zidon, and dwell there; behold, I have commanded a widow woman there to sustain thee. So he arose and went to Zarephath. And when he came to the gate of the city, behold, the widow woman was there gathering of sticks: and he called to her, and said, Fetch me, I pray thee, a little water in a vessel, and I may drink. And as she was going to fetch it, he called to her, and said, Bring me, I pray thee, a morsel of bread in thine hand. And she said, As the Lord thy God liveth, I have not a cake, but an handful of meal in a barrel, and a little oil in a cruse: and, behold, I am gathering two sticks, that I may go in and dress it for me and my son, that we may eat it, and die. And Elijah said unto her, Fear not, go and do as thou hast said: but make me thereof a little cake first, and bring it unto me, and after make for thee and for thy son. For thus saith the Lord God of Israel, The barrel of meal shall not waste, neither shall the cruse of oil fail, until the day that the Lord sendeth rain upon the earth. And she went and did according to the saying of Elijah: and she, and he, and her house, did eat many days. And the barrel of meal wasted not, neither did the cruse of oil fail, according to the word of the Lord, which he spake by Elijah. (I Kings 17:8-16.)

Do you think that really happened? I do. I believe it because I have learned that it happens in any day when anyone lives by the secret rule hidden here. True, it does sound impossible. You couldn't be blamed if you joined the scoffers who cry, "Miracles like that don't come off anymore."

But they do. I've seen them come true and I hope they will come true for you. So, will you take these six words of our title, place them deep in your heart much like a woman puts yeast in her dough, and let them work an expanding glory in your life? Here they are: "Make me a little cake first."

That's what the prophet said to the woman. That's what she did and it blessed her, it blessed her son, and it blessed the Lord.

There are some questions which come from a study of the text.

1. *Do you possess your possessions, or do your possessions possess you?*

When Elijah met the widow of Zarephath, she was fast in the clutch of a handful of meal and a wee bit of oil.

We sympathize with her. This is one lone woman against a famined land. For weeks she has been watching the flour barrel go down and this is the day of the dead end. Anyone who reads this is touched by the morbid story. Our heart goes out to her.

So did the prophet's heart. But he knew something which she didn't know. He knew that the way to have what you have, and to have it to the fullest is to put God first. That's why he said, "Make me a little cake first."

She did. "She went and did according to the saying of Elijah,

101

and she, and he, and her house, did eat many days." One little woman put God first and there went her fear. When she refused to be had by what little she had, great things took place through her.

2. *Is yours a healthy attitude toward the future? Does tomorrow pinch and bind you, or do you look forward with high anticipation to the days to come?*

The widow of Zarephath was searching for two sticks. She was concentrating on one last frugal meal. She was expecting death.

Again, we do not chide her. All about her, people were hungry and her neighbors may have been dying one by one. The days ahead were bleak by earthly expectations.

This is not true for most of us. Thank goodness there are very few people in our homes whose tomorrows are that foreboding. One way or another, most of us will eat.

But the future, and our attitude toward it, is a vital concern. In our day we often fall into the trap of thinking that when we get more money six months from now, when our bank account is built up three years hence, then our worries will be over.

Does your budget make you nervous? Do your bills loom large against payday? Are you frightened as you consider your income over against your outgo? "No," you may say, "I never worry about finances." Congratulations to you. Sit patiently then while the rest of us muse on this: We either worry about money or we don't, and the difference is not in the amount which we hold in our hand. The simple truth is that fear is multiplied, not diminished, by the acquisition of goods. Any keen observer of life knows that the more we get, the more we are prone to become fidgety. Cash in the bank does not free us from concern. It is likely to step up, rather than decrease, our worry.

Jesus talked much about a man and his possessions. He had only three years to teach. Why did he spend so much valuable time on money? It was because he knew the human mind as no one ever knew the human mind. He knew we would be prone to reason, "When I get more of those great big, beautiful dollars then I'll relax and enjoy life, then I'll be more generous, then I will be free in my giving."

But Christ also knew that this is not so. He must have known that the day would come when for many men the dividend would be god and six percent would be his prophet. He knew, likewise, that when we have danced too long before the golden calf, we are powerless to do otherwise.

Jesus knew that this would be a growing problem in each individual life which did not put the heavenly Father first.

This is the key to conquering our future. We end our fear of the days to come whenever we do as the widow did. We rise high above the storms of today and tomorrow whenever we live by these great words: "Make me a little cake first."

3. Comes now another question which requires an answer: *Don't you really think that God has enough in his storehouses for your needs?*

God loves us. Jesus says he does. If then he loves us, knows what is good for us, wants us to have his best, why wouldn't it make sense to put him first and operate all of life that way?

Answer: It does make sense. It made glorious good sense for the widow and it will make sense for us.

It says here: "And she went and did according to the saying."

She went and did. There is a real word: She did! God doesn't expect us to lie on our backs while he drops the food in our mouths. He has given us strength and health; he has blessed us with mind and judgment; he has equipped us with feet and hands; he has assigned us work in his kingdom, and he expects an honest accounting in personal stewardship.

He expects us to do our best. But when we do our best, he always does us better.

The widow was not up to her finest self and that stands out all over the story. She was at her worst. Life had her down. Her hope was gone and doubtless her energies had been depleted by her gloomy musings.

This all came about because she was centering her thoughts on what little she had rather than on the abundance of the heavenly Father who waited to bless her. It says very plainly that she was thinking of her wee supply rather than the fullness of the Lord. With no attempt to point the finger of scorn, we quickly observe that here was "poverty complex" at its ragged end. The undertones were of man's worst rather than God's best.

Elijah's great contribution to this woman was that he called her to lift her eyes above the narrow confines of her own little flour barrel to the amazing opulence of the Lord God Almighty.

These words can do the same for you: "Make me a little cake first!" If you will write this sentence on your heart and live by it, you too will know the thrill which comes from first turning the mind to God in all things.

Our church believes in percentage giving. We heartily recommend that all our members covenant with the Lord for a definite percent of their income. We urge our families to begin some-where and go on as God calls them on.

This is not all. We ask that our people always make out their check to God's work first. If you are paid in cash we believe you are wise to put your promised amount in your church envelope first. If you do business by check we urge that you write the check for your pledged percentage before you put your pen to any other account.

In all you do, in things big and little, we hold that the way to live is to put the Lord first and let all of life relate itself to that commitment.

When you have learned to do this in small ways and large, you can believe this word of the Book. For when you do it, you have put yourself in the path of the onrushing love of God. Now the whole universe is free to meet your need. Now your life is working partnership with the Lord and you will know that this is not a tale, it is living truth: "And she went and did according to the saying of Elijah: and the barrel of meal wasted not, neither did the cruse of oil fail, according to the word of the Lord."

XI

Seed Thoughts for Development

THE PRINCIPLE OF GOD'S OWNERSHIP

LIFE BELONGS TO GOD. THIS IS THE VERY KEYNOTE UNDER THE existence of the world itself. God created and owns all we have. God has given us life to be used for him. Just as a banker calls in a loan when it is due, so God himself can call us to surrender the principle, and no court in the land, nor statute, nor even the favorite motion, "Mr. Chairman, I move this matter be laid on the table for later consideration," nor any other maneuver can be of assistance when he calls for an accounting of our stewardship.

The Owner has been very fair. He does not place in man this feeling of obligation and leave him to guess the way. Neither has God given his children criteria completely unrelated to everyday existence. He has made it easy for man to measure his devotion at some points. From the earliest records of our faith, God said, "I'll take one-seventh of your time—'remember the seventh day to keep it holy.' I'll take one-tenth of your material goods—'Bring ye all your tithes.'"

In the New Testament Church, he directed his people to set aside a regular commitment as God prospered them. Christ calls men to give his all in recognition of God's ownership of all. Percentage giving is a practical symbol of the spiritual understanding that our life is not our own.

MAMMON

Christ did not allow any happy medium when he talked about mammon—"mammon" means money, and our Lord does not quibble, nor rationalize. He leaves no side doors open here. He did not say, "Ye *must* not serve God and mammon." His words were not tempered with, "It *is inadvisable* to serve God and mammon." What he said was, "Ye *cannot* serve God and mammon." This is an unyielding statement like, "You can't walk east and west at the same time." Christ knew that the man who tried to walk two ways at once is bound to tear somewhere.

In the old melodrama, the highwayman jumped from the bushes and shouted, "Your money or your life." Today, the approach is much more subtle. Our souls are seldom lost in one big chunk. Usually the loss is "here a little, there a little."

At first John and Mary were poor and they fought it through side by side. They wanted new things together but, since they had little money, they stayed at home fixing scrapbooks and "just talking." They worked in the church and sought Christian fellowship with other couples like themselves.

Then John came home with a pay raise and they were thrilled, then came another, and another. Now they were "free." Today he's doing extremely well as a true "comer" in his company. But Mary is building up to a nervous breakdown, and John is spending more and more time away from home. They're going faster and faster now in search of more freedom, less discipline, and new satisfactions.

What is the matter? They are living without commitment to anything higher than their own high time. Their major goal now is to "free" themselves more. They keep up a token interest in the church. They wouldn't want to live in a community without churches. They even have a recognition pledge to the annual budget.

But Jesus was right, "Ye *cannot* serve God and mammon."

One way to guard against being weaned away from life with the Lord is to live by specific rules which apply at any scale. The Old Testament law of the tithe and the New Testament recommendation to proportionate giving are for our good as well as the Lord's.

The Galatians 5:22-23 Test

Question: Should all my tithes and offerings be to the church?

Answer: This is for each individual to decide, but here is a good rule: Give to whatever represents Kingdom building in your life. There is an excellent test for people and projects, organizations and movements, individuals and groups, to see if they qualify as Kingdom builders. It is called the "Galatians 5:22-23 test": "But the fruit of the Spirit is love, joy, peace, long-suffering, gentleness, goodness, faith, meekness, temperance." Are the channels which seek your tithes and offerings producing these fruits?

If You Can't See How

One of our tithers says, "When we promised to tithe, my wife and I didn't see how we could do it. We didn't realize it then, but this is one of the secrets. The tither who sees how he can do it is bound to be missing something. Promising the Lord ten per cent before we get it provides the magic thrill which is sure to follow such a commitment." The Bible says, "But without faith it is impossible to please him: for he that cometh to God must believe that he is, and that he is a rewarder of them that diligently seek him" (Heb. 11:6).

QUOTES from unknown authors:

God is always seeking good stewards. When he finds them he uses them by giving them more to use for him.

Careless giving always leads to "care-less" living.

When you ask, "What will tithing do *to* my finances?" change the question and meditate on this: "What will tithing do *for* my finances?"

The man who says, "I can't give more. I'm in debt," should ask himself, "Am I not also in debt to God?"

When things master a man, they enslave him. When God masters a man, he emancipates him.

A father, through insurance, can provide money for education and for emergencies. Training in regular, systematic giving is insurance for keeping a child close to the Lord and growing in character.

RIGHT STEWARDSHIP DOES MANY THINGS

1. *It ushers in the real joy of the Lord to the deep places of our soul.*

109

In the parable of the talents, do you remember what the Lord said to the man who made a good stewardship of life? Was it, "Well done, thou good and faithful servant, enter thou into the bank vaults of the Lord and draw out whatever you like"? Of course not. The words are: "Enter thou *into the joy* of thy Lord."

If your inner contentment runs low at times and if you have that dull feeling more than you want; if your heart is heavy often, and you feel low when you want to feel glad, you may find the reason in your pocketbook. Always, Christian stewardship brings with it the deep glow of Christian gladness.

Right stewardship does many things for us.

2. *It assists us in the destruction of jealousy.*

The Bible says, "Jealousy is cruel as the grave: the coals thereof are coals of fire, which hath a most vehement flame" (Song of S. 8:6). Most of us know this to be true. We have learned it the hard way. It is a fortunate person who can honestly say, "Envy has never been a problem with me."

Squaring our accounts with God can work a mighty assist in this connection. This is true because it teaches us to look to God for our supply. Life with him will show us that there is enough in the universe for us and for the other fellow also. Now we can rejoice at the good fortune of others, and we will not fuss. We know that we are living by the Father's rules and that our goodness will come to us in his good time as we have need.

Right stewardship of our money does many things for us.

3. *It is an aid in increasing our efficiency.*

An editor who began tithing wrote: "My desk was famous as the office eyesore. I have noticed that when I ordered my life even a little, by making a covenant with God for a set percent of my income, it had its effect on other areas. Even before I realized it, my fellow workers commented that my work table and my desk top showed that something had happened to me."

The Bible admonishes, "Let all things be done decently and in order" (I Cor. 14:40). Tithing, when it is a commitment made from the heart out, has a way of flowing up through our lives to order our ways.

Christ-directed giving does many things for us.

4. *It helps us to master our natural tendency to selfishness.*

It is said that one of Pietro Mascagni's operas is inscribed with this dedication: "To myself with distinguished esteem and unalterable satisfaction." Most of us shrink from such outright ego, but the facts are that we may have similar dedications written somewhere in our lives. Psychologists say that selfishness is one of the major causes of neurosis. An ancient wisdom writer, setting down his observations of life, said, "There is a sore evil which I have seen under the sun, namely, riches kept for the owners thereof to their hurt" (Eccl. 5:13). One way to defeat this proclivity is to adopt certain practices which force us to turn our lives out rather than in.

Right stewardship does many things for us.

5. *It gives us the solid satisfaction that we are being useful.*

The scriptures talk often of "purpose." They tell us of Daniel's purpose and Paul's. They speak of the purpose of Christ and the purposes of God. They admonish us, "Every man according as he purposeth in his heart, so let him give" (II Cor. 9:7).

111

Many people are bored because they have no large reasons for living. They are wearied from serving false gods.

What is the purpose of life? It is not to make the world better, although that is good. It isn't to have a fine family and build a good home, though this also has real merit. It isn't for us to help one another along life's way, fine as that may be. The purpose of life isn't even to find the Lord. *He has already found us* and this is basic to all our thinking. He waits outside our heart's door in the presence of Christ. He waits outside every little heart door within us, the surface doors and the doors to those faraway chambers of our soul. The purpose of life is to be found of God for his purposes.

Regular, systematic, Christian giving takes us away from using to being used. It creates in us a frame of mind whereby we recognize that we were made to be God's channel through which his blessing can flow to all his world.

Appendix I

Copy of brochure as indicated in Chapter IV. This piece is given to new members on the day they join the church. It is made available at the literature rack and church office for prospects and members who wish to distribute it to those considering membership. The pastor and officers refer to it frequently in their discussions both public and individual.

COUNTING THE COST

YOUR STEWARDSHIP CHALLENGE

AT

MEMORIAL DRIVE PRESBYTERIAN CHURCH

"And whosoever doth not bear his cross, and come after me, cannot be my disciple. For which of you, intending to build a tower, sitteth not down first, and counteth the cost."

—Luke 14:27-28

Jesus said:

"Thou shalt love the Lord thy God with all thy heart, and with all thy soul, and with all thy mind. This is the first and great commandment."

—Matt. 22:37

One of the boys in our church school, upon hearing this verse, said, "He didn't miss a thing, did he?" We believe that Christian stewardship doesn't miss a thing. Christ expects us to surrender all we are and all we have to his service.

Therefore the first official word of your church on Christian giving is: *Let the Lord direct you!*

Your new Church believes that you can best do this by *percentage giving*. Perhaps this is an entirely new concept for you.

What do we mean? Here is our definition!

A PERCENTAGE GIVER

One who covenants with God to give to the kingdom causes a set percentage of all he receives.

He pays that percentage first from all that comes into his hands.

By study of God's word and by daily life with the risen Lord, he keeps his heart open to increasing his percentage as Christ leads him to further commitments.

We believe this practice is true to the teaching of the New Testament Church. The apostle Paul instructed his people, "Upon the first day of the week let every man lay by him in store as God hath prospered him" (I Cor. 16:2).

Based on this approach, our official motto is: "We are not concerned with your share of our budget—what really matters is God's share of your income."

We really mean that we would rather you covenant with the Lord for a set percentage of all that comes into your hand than for you to give now what you think is a generous pledge. We hold that when you practice percentage giving you have put yourself in a position to grow in grace as the Lord leads you on.

(Naturally, we expect you to indicate on your pledge card approximately how much your new percentage giving approach will come to. It is important for the deacons to know the total pledges of all our people in order to manage the Church's affairs.) Individual pledges are kept confidential in our church and are a matter between the giver, the Lord and the church treasurer. This is done, not for protection, but in order to make it the sacred matter which it should be between God and the giver.

Percentage giving always leads to questions on the age-old practice of tithing. Our goal is to become a tithing congregation.

Let's take a look at:

WHAT WE MEAN BY A TITHING CHURCH

A Congregation where a majority of families:
  I. Have studied the tithe as a directive from God to his people in the Old Testament.
 II. Have recognized the tithe as a rich blessing to a multitude of Christians who have made it their practice.
III. Have opened their own ears to what Christ the Living Word has to say to them personally concerning this matter.
IV. Have recognized proportionate giving as a New Testament mode of financial stewardship.
 V. Are practicing percentage giving as a symbol of Christ's lordship and as a specific means of growing in grace.

Notice very carefully that we do not believe tithing is the ultimate in Christian giving. We do not say that you must be a tither before you can be a full follower of Christ. Actually, you may not yet be ready to begin tithing. The truth is that you may one day be led beyond this level.

This is the important factor—What does God want from you?

We want you to clearly understand that we do not think you can be what you should be as a member of our church until you have settled your stewardship between you and the Christ who gave his all for you!

We hope you will pray this prayer: Lord show me what to do—and I will do it!

Toward this end Memorial Drive Church has a carefully developed long-range plan of Christian stewardship training. Weekly in your church service bulletin you will find a notice on this matter. Quarterly in our church-school you and your children will hear a speaker on this subject. Twice annually you will receive a letter from the officers, and twice each year our pastor delivers a sermon on some phase of the giving theme. These references which you will see and hear are not casually tossed into the general teaching of the church. They are a part of a carefully laid plan to bring you closer to the Master through your personal commitment of time, talents, and money. We urge you to keep an open mind and to develop a prayerful heart toward these teachings. We say it again, "We do not believe that you can be that kind of member which Christ needs in this church unless you remain open to divine direction."

God early promised rich rewards for those who right their lives with his will. We want you to experience the deep satisfaction and the abundant blessings which are sure to follow whenever men surrender their hearts and follow where his Son leads in the Kingdom.

It is our prayer that this Church's stewardship training may open up new joys and a thrilling new way of life to you and your family.

The second big fact which we hope you will face as a member of this church is that our budget is no ordinary thing. Chances are you have never been in a congregation with responsibilities as heavy as your new ones here.

Memorial Drive Presbyterian is a dollar-for-dollar benevolence church. This puts a tremendous new stewardship responsibility squarely on your shoulders. This program means that for each dollar spent on our operating funds a matching dollar goes to causes outside our local congregation. It means that fifty cents out of your dollar goes to educate a student for the ministry in America, to heal a native in the Belgian Congo, or to tell someone somewhere about your Lord. We hope this fact will grow on you until it becomes a dynamic experience in your life. You will find before you have been with us long that your fellow church members would give up almost anything before parting with this sacred trust.

This is not easy. Sometimes it hurts. Sometimes it means that we do not have the things we want. Sometimes it means that we must go without items, without activities, and without staff members which would be considered absolute essentials in other churches. But Christ never promised that life would be easy for those who do his will and we do not expect it otherwise for us.

Since this is our challenge and our privilege you will want to help us face this fact:

It costs much more per capita to operate Memorial Drive Church than it does to operate other churches. Since our congregation has undertaken building the Kingdom, it means that each one of us has extra responsibility!

Very often new members say, "But what is my share?"

Our answer is, "Your share is what God asks you to do for him!"

To help you decide what God wants you to do, we know you

will want to look at some revealing figures. An outline of our budget in a recent year looked like this—(detailed copies of this year's figures are available for you at the church office)

Total Budget 117,960
Total Operating 58,980
Total Benevolences 58,980

(The operating fund includes such items as salaries, insurance, utilities, literature, postage, social activities, youth work, church school, music, nursery expenses and general supplies.)

This does not include the building fund which is a separate item.

Our board has estimated that we require a certain amount each week but does this mean that you must give this much before you are doing your share as a member of Memorial Drive Church?

It most certainly does not. But it does mean that you now hold membership in a church which has tremendous demands from the Lord to carry on his work. He has no other way to accomplish his program here except as each of us seriously *faces up to this:* The holy calling of this church to its dollar-for-dollar benevolences, plus other ordinary costs, plus providing a building for our use, must be borne by each one of us asking God to show us his rightful share of our income in our new relationship.

When you have laid these facts on your heart and prayerfully considered them, we hope you will join us often in this prayer:

Lord I am grateful for a church which constantly challenges me to realign my life with Christ in every way. I want to carry my end of the work. But keep me aware that my share in this church's budget will take care of itself if I take care to give you your share of my income. May I be a Christ-led steward of all my life. Show me what to do—and I will do it! Amen.

Appendix II

Front

MY PLEDGE
IN SUPPORT OF

The Memorial Drive Presbyterian Church
HOUSTON, TEXAS

In grateful recognition of the spiritual benefits received from my church and as an evidence of my interest in its work and in the extension of the Kingdom, I hereby promise to pay to the church treasurer the sum of $_____ during the period _____, 19__ to _____, 19__, payable _____ weekly, _____ monthly, _____ quarterly.

Sign here

Address

Date _____

This subscription, being wholly voluntary, may be increased, decreased, or canceled, at any time, upon written notice to the church treasurer.

(OVER)

Back

Your church's approach to stewardship urges the practice of "percentage giving."

A percentage giver is one who:

1. Covenants between himself and God to give a certain percentage of all he receives to Kingdom causes;

2. Gives this amount first; and

3. Keeps an open heart toward his church's teaching on tithing, seeking to grow toward the scriptural standard of giving.

I am glad to practice percentage giving. . . .

___ Yes   ___ No   ___ Cannot

Appendix III

Listed below are the denominational offices of churches affiliated with the Commission on Stewardship and Benevolence of the National Council of Churches of Christ in the U.S.A. This office of the council itself has some material on stewardship training. The addresses given are those of the departments of benevolence or stewardship of each member church.

African Methodist Episcopal Church, 3526 Dodier, St. Louis, MO 63107

American Baptist Churches in the U.S.A., Valley Forge, PA 19481.

Christian Church (Disciples of Christ), P.O. Box 1986, Indianapolis, IN 46206.

Church of the Brethren, 1451 Dundee Avenue, Elgin, IL 60120.

The Episcopal Church, 815 Second Avenue, New York, NY 10017.

Friends United Meeting, 101 Quaker Hill Drive, Richmond, IN 47374.

Greek Orthodox Archdiocese of North and South America, 10 East 79th Street, New York, NY 10021.

Lutheran Church in America, 2900 Queen Lane, Philadelphia, PA 19129.

Moravian Church in America, Northern Province, P.O. Box 1245, Bethlehem, PA 18018.

Presbyterian Church in the U.S., 341 Ponce de Leon Avenue NE, Atlanta, GA 30308.

Reformed Church in America, 475 Riverside Drive, New York, NY 10027.

United Church of Christ, 1505 Race Street, Philadelphia, PA 19102.

The United Methodist Church, Division of Evangelism, Worship, and Stewardship, Board of Discipleship, Box 840, Nashville, TN 37202.

The United Presbyterian Church in the U.S.A., 475 Riverside Drive, New York, NY 10027.

CANADA

The Anglican Church of Canada, 600 Jarvis Street, Toronto, Ontario M4Y2J6.

The Baptist Convention of Ontario and Quebec, 217 St. George Street, Toronto, Ontario M5R2M2.

The Baptist Union of Western Canada, 4404 16th Street SW, Calgary, Alberta T2T4H9.

The Presbyterian Church in Canada, 50 Wynford Drive, Don Mills, Ontario M3C1J7.

The United Church of Canada, 85 St. Clair Avenue E, Toronto, Ontario M4T1M8.

United Baptist Convention of the Atlantic Provinces, Box 7053 Station A, St. John, New Brunswick E2L4S5.

NON-MEMBER DENOMINATIONS

The American Lutheran Church, 422 South Fifth Street, Minneapolis, MN 55415

Church of God (Anderson, Indiana), P.O. Box 2420, Anderson, IN 46011.

Churches of God, General Conference, P.O. Box 926, Findlay, OH 45840.

Cumberland Presbyterian Church, P.O. Box 4149, Memphis, TN 38104.

The Evangelical Covenant Church of America, 5101 North Francisco Avenue, Chicago, IL 60625.

Lutheran Church—Missouri Synod, 500 North Broadway, St. Louis, MO 63102.

Mennonite Church, The General Board, 528 East Madison Street, Lombard, IL 60148.

Mennonite Church, The General Conference, P.O. Box 347, Newton, KS 67114.

Reorganized Church of Jesus Christ of Latter Day Saints, The Auditorium, Box 1059, Independence, MO 64051.

Seventh-day Adventists, 6840 Eastern Avenue NW, Washington, DC 20012.